Journey Into Spirit Life

Finding Purpose, Power And Peace In The Kingdom

Gary Brown and Pam Fox

Journey Into Spirit Life

Copyright © 2008 by Gary Brown and Pam Fox

All rights reserved. No part of this book may be reproduced without written permission of the authors.

Scripture quotations are taken from the King James Version of the Holy Bible unless otherwise noted.

Scripture quotations marked "NKJV™" are taken from the New King James Version®. Copyright © 1982 by Thomas Nelson, Inc. Used by permission. All rights reserved.

Scripture quotations marked (NIV) are taken from the HOLY BIBLE, NEW INTERNATIONAL VERSION®. NIV®. Copyright© 1973, 1978, 1984 by International Bible Society. Used by permission of Zondervan. All rights reserved.

Spirit Life Publishing
11901 S. Hwy 96
Greenwood, AR 72936
479-353-2219

Journey Into Spirit Life is dedicated to our spouses, Tim Fox and Teresa Brown. Without their confidence and encouragement, the book would not have been possible.

Introduction

This is a book about living life in Christ. This book is for believers in any season of their journey who want full abundance promised in Christ. For believers who want to reach the mark of their high calling in Christ Jesus. Believers who want to live the Christian life to the fullest, finding their place in the Kingdom. This book is about *righteousness, peace and joy in the Holy Ghost.* Jesus said *"I am come that you might have life, and that you might have it more abundantly."* Many believers long for that abundance in their lives but never know how to reach it, often fruitlessly struggling for it in their *flesh.* We think that, after reading JOURNEY INTO SPIRIT LIFE, you will agree this is not merely a retelling of the tri-part man teaching. We believe you will find fresh understanding here which will help you in your journey toward maturity and fullness in Christ.

We will focus on overcoming the unbalanced emotions and desires of man through faith and on becoming believers who are living out of the dominance of the human spirit submitted to Christ. **If God's children were set free from unbalanced, excessive emotion and misguided desires, God's Kingdom would be greatly advanced in believers and, therefore, upon the earth.** God sent His Son that all might have life and have it more abundantly. The quenching of the human spirit to magnify the soul and body brings glory to self and hinders the fullness of God's plan in most believers. **The greatest veil is the veil of unbalanced, soulish emotion and the greatest freedom is a spirit set free to reign over the life of the believer.**

There is a place beyond tradition, religion, and human reasoning where God desires to take us. We can go there only by grace through faith. In other words, we can go there only by **God's grace** through **God's faithfulness**. God, in His *faithful* commitment to intimacy with His creation, *graciously* sent Jesus to make provision for that intimacy. Most believers will acknowledge this as truth but stop far short of the sufficiency of grace that is found in Christ. There is a place in the Kingdom of God called "deep unto deep". It is where revelation of the mysteries of the Kingdom flow, a place where the uncommon becomes common. **It is a place where you are rooted in the agape' heart of God (His love) and, as you live in this place, your confidence of purpose grows along with the assurance of God's love.** Fear and insecurity melt away. Grace and peace are multiplied and JOY explodes. This is a place of Spirit. It is a place the natural mind does not fathom. The Spirit of the Living God draws us to this place of intimate relationship as we come into agreement and cooperation with the Spirit of God through our faith, patience, abandonment and trust. **Believing God's Word *absolutely* is the part we play in cooperating with the work of the Spirit in our lives.**

Let's begin by looking at some classic definitions to which we will adhere throughout this book:

body - The body is the container in which our spirit and soul are deposited. It is the physical shell in which we function. Pretty important, huh? God formed the body from dirt and it was lifeless.

soul - The soul is our mind. It contains our emotions, our reasoning and our will. We may think of the soul as the mind or brain. It is our thought process. It defines who we are, our personality. Man became a *living* soul when the breath of God was breathed into that clay body. Genesis 2:7 says precisely that: *And the LORD God formed man [of] the dust of the ground, and breathed into his nostrils the breath of life; and man became a living soul.*

spirit - The spirit is the breath of God. It is the spirit that gives life (John 6:63). Without the spirit, there is no life. The spirit is the **human spirit** breathed into man by God. This is not the Holy Spirit but the human spirit. When the spirit was breathed into the body of man, man became a living soul. In other words, the body is impregnated by the breath or spirit and the soul is produced. Man then becomes a tri-part being of spirit, soul and body.

flesh - We will refer to flesh as the *cooperation between the body and the soul*. The body often responds, for example, to the emotions and reasoning of the soul and cooperates to live out the fruit of that reasoning. We call that the will of man. For example, your body feels tired, your emotions are on edge, you reason that you must have rest, and your body cooperates to lie down and sleep. Cooperation of soul and body can be a normal, healthy function. Often, however, our emotions and reasoning go astray and veer outside of God's plan for our lives, even into those areas deemed as sin and harmful to man. The body can be quite cooperative in those areas as well!

Man is made of these three parts: spirit, soul and body. Those three elements make up man as shown in the illustration below. The heart represents man's spirit, the flame represents man's soul and the outline of a man represents the body which contains the spirit and soul. These three parts make up man.

Now imagine man's spirit, soul and body as three gears as illustrated. For now, please accept our premise that, while all three are vital, the spirit is the most significant part of man, the soul is the middle part and the body is the lowest part. So, the big gear represents the spirit, the mid-size gear represents the soul and the small gear represents the body. Imagine that you crank the large, "spirit" gear, making it the dominant gear which turns the others. You can turn it with little effort and struggle. The soul and body hum right along at fast speed. But try to keep up the same pace by turning the small gears. Crank the "body" gear and you will have to use much more effort to keep your "spirit" gear spinning at its original speed. Likewise, the middle or "soul" gear will have to be cranked with more effort to keep the "spirit" gear at a speed consistent with its original speed. When the small or middle gears are usually the driving or dominant gears, the energy expended to keep the large gear turning at the original speed will be great. Growing tired, you will have to slow down, never reaching full potential speed and efficiency. When the large, "spirit" gear is the dominant driving gear, less energy will be expended and the whole gear mechanism will work more efficiently at a higher speed.

Have you seen the "before and after" pictures on the internet or on billboards of young men or women on meth? In the first picture, they appear healthy. In the second picture, after only a couple of years on meth, they appear to have aged thirty or forty years. The emotional and physical desire of their soul and body drives them to meth and they become addicted. It seems their spirit has been totally suppressed. Exactly! You may have heard it said of someone, "it seems their spirit is broken". God intended that man live out of the abundance of a healthy spirit.

Admittedly, this is an extreme and graphic example of someone who gives total control to their flesh. However, most believers, indeed most all people, live their life out of the unbalanced excess of their soul and body (emotion and desire) rather than out of the abundance of their spirit. This creates a dilemma because God intended that man's spirit be dominant, ruled by His Word. The soul and body, known as flesh, are to be submissive and work in harmony with spirit. Ideally, the human spirit works in harmony with the Holy Spirit. The flesh then works in harmony with the human spirit. Together, in the progress of this book, let us *reckon ourselves* to be alive unto God through Jesus Christ (Romans 6:11). The Greek word for "alive" means *to have true, active, blessed, endless, vital, fresh, vigorous, powerful, efficient life*. We are commanded to *reckon ourselves* to be that alive!

Is that the life you desire? Do you want to know your place in the Kingdom of God more fully? Do you want to progressively look more like your Heavenly Father, living out the truth that you are "created in His image"? Do you want to be everything He intends you to be, living effectually and powerfully? Do you want to know the fullness of God's plan for your life? Do you want to give Him glory by your *vital, active, powerful, vigorous life* in Christ?

We pray that all who read this book will receive revelation by the Holy Spirit. It is possible to read every word, feel you have been blessed with good information and continue with life as usual. On the other hand, you can receive the information here along with revelation by the Spirit. **Revelation brings revolution in your life, affecting transformation.** This is revelation which transforms you progressively into the image of your Heavenly Father. **It is the Holy Spirit's responsibility to work transformation in your life by God's Word** *when you cooperate with the will of God*, bringing you *purpose, power* *and peace.* Cooperating with the will of God is something we will discuss more fully later. For now, suffice it to say that cooperating with God's will is *trusting the Holy Spirit to work God's promise in you.* A few more definitions:

Purpose is *God's will or pleasure in your life.*

Power is *the Word of God working in you by the Holy Spirit, enabling you to live out God's purpose.*

Peace is *the fruit of purpose and power.* When you live out purpose, you will live in peace.

USING THE TRI-PART BEING

Scientists have long explained that we use only a tiny portion of our brain, some using less than others (you know those people, right?). The same could be said for the *bodies* of most men and women. However, look at the athlete who has pushed his body to a more full *potential.* Look at the brilliant scholar who has pressed his mind toward its *potential.* We do not deny that man has neglected full potential of mind and body but contend that man has, nonetheless, given a tremendous amount of attention to the completion and adornment of the body and to inputting knowledge into our brain or soul. Man also uses the soul, the mind, to contain enormous amounts of emotion. That emotion and our knowledge of life result in reasoning and that reasoning determines our decisions or will. The body, when cooperative, then lives out that will. **We contend that, if indeed we use our soul (mind) and body at far less than their potential (and we do), we must use the spirit to even less degree of potential. Man's spirit must be the most neglected part of the tri-part being.** How much time do we spend developing the spirit?

*For they that are after the flesh (*body + soul*) do mind the things of the flesh; but they that are after the Spirit the things of the Spirit. For to be carnally (*concentrating on the flesh*) minded [is] death; but to be spiritually minded [is] life and peace.* –Romans 8:5-6

We become "spiritually minded" by allowing the development of our spirit to become dominant over our soul and body. In the perfected or matured believer, the spirit is dominant over flesh, resulting in more abundant life, bringing a greater balance to your tri-part man in spirit, soul and body.

We are not contending that *absolute perfection* can be achieved in the earthly realm. We do, however, contend that believers have set their sights far too low and can achieve a much higher plane of maturity or perfection in their spirit than typically anticipated. We will sometimes refer to this maturity as **perfected love.**

The mind of sinful man is death, but the mind controlled by the Spirit is life and peace; the sinful mind is hostile to God. It does not submit to God's law, nor can it do so. Those controlled by the sinful nature cannot please God. You, however, are controlled not by the sinful nature but by the Spirit, if the Spirit of God lives in you. And if anyone does not have the Spirit of Christ, he does not belong to Christ. But if Christ is in you, your body is dead because of sin, yet your spirit is alive because of righteousness. And if the Spirit of him who raised Jesus from the dead is living in you, he who raised Christ from the dead will also give life to your mortal bodies through his Spirit, who lives in you. Therefore, brothers, we have an obligation—but it is not to the sinful nature, to live according to it. For if you live according to the sinful nature, you will die; but if by the Spirit you put to death the misdeeds of the body, you will live, because those who are led by the Spirit of God are sons of God. For you did not receive a spirit that makes you a slave again to fear, but you received the Spirit of sonship. And by him we cry, "Abba, Father." The Spirit himself testifies with our spirit that we are God's children. –Romans 8:6-16 NIV

When a person believes on Jesus and is reconciled to God by the blood of Jesus, that person becomes a *child of God*. There would be those who would argue that all mankind are in a general sense, by virtue of being His creation, children of God. However, we speak of a more specific spiritual adoption into the family of God through belief on Jesus.

*For you did not receive a spirit that makes you a slave again to fear, but you received the Spirit of sonship. And by him we cry, "Abba, Father." The **Spirit himself testifies with our spirit** that we are God's children. –Romans 8:15-16 NIV*

Notice here in Romans 8, that the Spirit (<u>capital S means Holy Spirit</u>) is working in cooperation with the human spirit to assure the believer of their adoption into God's family!

There is maturing process in the *young or underdeveloped believer*. Some call it *sanctification*. Some call it *perfecting*. We are the sons of God when we believe. As we mature in our spirit, led or taught by the Holy Spirit, we begin to look more and more like our Heavenly Father and are more easily recognized as a child of God. This journey into perfection is accomplished the same way we received our salvation. First, we heard the Word of God. "Faith comes by hearing and hearing by the Word of God." We were then drawn by or convicted by the Holy Spirit that we needed a Savior. Finally, we responded by believing the Word and accepting the blood sacrifice of Jesus. We asked forgiveness of sin and chose to make Him Lord of our life. We were born again! Not accustomed to that "born again" terminology? Look at this:

Therefore if any man [be] in Christ, [he is] a new creature: old things are passed away; behold, all things are become new. -2 Cor. 5:17

This "birth" brought you into relationship with God the Father. You are "born again".

Jesus saith unto him, I am the way, the truth, and the life: no man cometh unto the Father, but by me. - John 14:6

This is the heart desire of the Father, to have deep, intimate relationship with His creation. We must also understand the very bedrock, the foundation, of God's plan both for salvation and ultimate fullness or maturity of salvation is rooted in His heart of love, the agape' heart of the Father. For God is love and all that He does comes from His love.

For God so loved the world, that he gave His only begotten Son, that whosoever believeth in Him should not perish, but have everlasting life. —John 3:16

For by grace are ye saved through faith; and that not of yourselves: [it is] the gift of God: Not of works, lest any man should boast. —Eph. 2: 8-9

Grace is the merciful kindness by which Jesus gives you His favor, exerting His holiness upon you that you might increase in the faith, knowledge and affections of the Father. Faith is trusting in God's faithfulness. It is God's ability, His faithfulness, not yours, that saves you. Read Ephesians 2: 8-9 again with that understanding.

*For by **grace** are ye saved through **faith**; and that not of yourselves: [it is] **the gift of God**: Not of works, lest any man should boast. –Eph. 2: 8-9*

Too few believers progress into the multiplication of grace that they might increase in faith, knowledge and affections of the Father. Grace and faith must go hand in hand; they are inseparable. We must continue in His grace and be a people who live by faith and not by sight (circumstance). Living by sight, by our earthly circumstances, will allow our emotions to dominate us! **The principle of agreement with God brings fullness or maturity, dominance of our spirit. Our faith is our agreement with God which brings the promises, benefits, pleasures, and purposes He has given for His and our pleasure (joy).** Faith is expressed and works in cooperation with the Holy Spirit in four ways. They are faith, patience, abandonment and trust. Our submission and obedience is the by-product of these four. If these are not alive in your life, you will never know fullness and maturity of the purpose God has ordained for you. You can have a car with a powerful engine, it can be fueled and ready to go, but unless you drive the car, getting behind the wheel in agreement with all that power, it will be unable to take you where you want to go. **Our faith, patience, abandonment and trust is the agreement God requires to take us into fullness or maturity**.

Someday, when Jesus returns for His church, we will graduate into **absolute fullness** as a son of God. We should **not use this truth** as an excuse for neglect of our spirit-man during our earthly journey.

The creation waits in eager expectation for the sons of God to be revealed. -Romans 8:19 NIV

Many believers, through lack of comprehension or revelation, are waiting for their death and literal passage into the presence of God or for the Second Coming for fullness when a large measure of fullness is available right now. Jesus said we should pray, "Thy Kingdom come, Thy will be done, on earth as it is in heaven". Just like the first disciples, we sometimes pray as if we expect God to physically lower His Kingdom upon the earth. Jesus, however, said the Kingdom of God is **without observation**, not being a visible kingdom, but that it is **within the believer.** He spoke just that to His disciples:

Once, having been asked by the Pharisees when the kingdom of God would come, Jesus replied, "The kingdom of God does not come with your careful observation, nor will people say, 'Here it is,' or 'There it is,' because the kingdom of God is within you."
-Luke 17:20-21 NIV

We are to mature into more complete (manifested) sons of God by the development of our spirit. The Holy Spirit is the teacher of our human spirit. That's why the scripture says:

But the anointing which ye have received of Him abideth in you, and ye need not that any man teach you: but as the same anointing teacheth you of all things, and is truth, and is no lie, and even as it hath taught you, ye shall abide in Him.
—I John 2:27

Through this book, you receive guidance toward finding your place in the Kingdom. Take this guidance and open your spirit to the inward teaching of the Holy Spirit. Take our scripture references, study them and the surrounding passages and pray that the Holy Spirit reveals the fullness of the Word to you. This function of the Holy Spirit quickens [*gives true, active, blessed, endless, vital, fresh, vigorous, powerful, efficient life to*] your mortal body. Your flesh is given fullness of life when your human spirit is cooperating with the Holy Spirit, resulting in purpose, power and peace!

But if the Spirit of Him that raised up Jesus from the dead dwell in you, He that raised up Christ from the dead shall also quicken your mortal bodies by his Spirit that dwelleth in you.
-Romans 8:11

You can live an abundant life. You can live out your full purpose of life as God intended. You do not have to be ruled out of unbalanced emotion and reasoning. You can know *spirit dominance* and "demand" that your soul and body come into cooperation with your spirit. The demanding is your faith *expressed*. By grace through faith, fullness of salvation, spirit dominance, comes just like our initial salvation. God's grace and faithfulness are constant. Our role is believing and cooperating with the working of God's Word in us by the Holy Spirit.

***Spirit dominance* is the human spirit submitted to the Teacher, the Holy Spirit, with flesh (soul and body) cooperating to the maturity of the believer and the glory of God.**

We will explore these truths more fully to a place of understanding and, by the help of the Holy Spirit, you will enter into a place of purpose, power and peace in the Kingdom of God.

Take your time while reading this book. If you try to read it through in one setting, you may become overwhelmed. There is a lot to "absorb" and the quest for spirit dominance can seem daunting for those who have struggled with their flesh. Your journey toward spirit dominance will be one step at a time. You may want to read the book one chapter at a setting; then, meditate on the truths expressed in that chapter. Some asked to preview the book integrated it into a "home group" study and the group studies one chapter during each group meeting.

Two questions for you: what could happen to the effectualness of a believer finding this place in God? What could happen in the effectualness of a church full of believers who have found their fullness in the Kingdom?

First Things First   Chapter One

Jesus taught the Kingdom. It was His central, core message. His parables illustrated Kingdom principles. In His sermon on the mount, recorded in Matthew 5, Jesus sets forth Kingdom citizen attributes in the first nine verses. Unfortunately, these attributes are largely ignored or understated in the modern church. If a new or renewed believer could receive only one teaching, *this is it.* If every believer embraced the truth contained within this one sermon of Jesus, the church would change the world "overnight". Let's take a fresh look at this greatest of Jesus' teachings.

And seeing the multitudes, He went up into a mountain: and when He was set, His disciples came unto Him: And He opened his mouth, and taught them, saying, Blessed [are] the poor in spirit: for theirs is the kingdom of heaven. –Matthew 5:1-3

Every believer, as the Kingdom grows inside and they are matured or perfected in their love, will mourn over their sin and over the corruption of the world by sin. This is a deep, abiding grief over personal sin and over the sins of the world. They weep compassionately over the sin of family members and friends. A believer who does not have or desire this spirit of mourning is, at best, an immature believer. If a spirit of mourning over sin *never comes even in small measure*, there is concern regarding their salvation. Believers mourn over sin. This spirit of mourning is often immature and underdeveloped in believers. We must embrace a mature spirit of mourning in order to be a good citizen of the Kingdom of God.

Blessed [are] the meek: for they shall inherit the earth. -Mat 5:5

Meekness is *strength under authority.* Meekness is surrendering your will to the authority of God. We do so with the understanding that God is watching out for our interests and will, indeed, give us the earth. The matured believer is confident that God is watching over his "territory". An immature believer is exhausting himself, protecting his territory, his stuff, his rights! Abraham meekly accepted God's plan and gave Lot the better land. His meekness was abundantly blessed of God and his territory became extremely fruitful (Gen. 13). While unredeemed man and even immature believers strive after power, riches and fame, the maturing citizen of God's Kingdom surrenders to God. God watches over and rewards his children who humbly live under His authority.

For My yoke [is] easy, and My burden is light. -Mat 11:30

Rabbis often facilitated the teaching of those young in their faith by teaming or yoking them with a seasoned person of the Jewish faith. On the Jewish farm, a young ox was placed in a yoke with a seasoned, mature beast. The mature beast became the authority. The young ox would learn from the older. To keep from chaffing and to find a better path, the young ox would learn to follow the slightest tug of the older beast. This prevented chaffing, lightened his load and taught him in the ways of the master. Likewise, we are supposed to be yoked with Jesus so we learn the slightest tug of His heart and follow immediately in obedience.

Blessed [are] they which do hunger and thirst after righteousness: for they shall be filled. -Mat 5:6

Righteousness defined simply is the "rightness" or character of God. As a believer desires the rightness of God, he is filled. This is the promise of God. Now, if you hunger for bread, what do you receive? Bread. If you hunger for righteousness, what will you receive? Righteousness. There is a scripture about seeking God's rightness in Matthew, chapter six:

But seek ye first the kingdom of God, and His righteousness; and all these things shall be added unto you. -Romans 6:33

In the preceding verses of Romans 6, we read that God will provide all of our material needs. *Your Heavenly Father knoweth that you have need of these [material] things* (verse 32b). Because we have just read the phrase, "these things", we link the same phrase in verse 33 to material things. However, *we contend* that "all these things" refers to those "things" *immediately spoken of in the **same verse**, verse 33.* In other words, if you seek first the kingdom of God and his righteousness, you will receive "all these things", the things being God's Kingdom and His righteousness. How important that a new or underdeveloped believer, indeed that EVERY believer seeking fullness understand this!

Blessed [are] the merciful: for they shall obtain mercy. –Mat. 5:7

We all need mercy. That's why the scripture describes *God's mercy as fresh every morning! (Lam. 3:23)* You will come to a time when you are in desperate need of God's mercy and, perhaps, the mercy of your fellow believer. At that time, you must look back upon a history of giving mercy that you might receive mercy. We reap what we sow. Sow mercy, reap mercy. If you must err, err on the side of mercy and not a heart of judgment. Wouldn't you prefer mercy over judgment in *your* time of need?

Blessed [are] the pure in heart: for they shall see God. -Mat 5:8

Perhaps there is no greater goal in the believer's life than seeing God. Seeing God's face (spiritually, not literally) is essential to the believer who wants to mature into the fullness of their Father. Simply put, if you are sincere in your heart toward God, He will reveal Himself to you. When you see God, you see His "wrinkles". In our earthly body, our face becomes more wrinkled as our struggles take their toll on us. If our struggles have resulted in spiritual growth, our wrinkles are trophies of that growth and, thereby, reveal that character. Now, we realize that is a very optimistic way to view wrinkles and that God doesn't have wrinkles, but work with us here, OK! Assuming the face reveals character, imagine seeing the character in God's face! Did you ever notice how, sometimes, the longer a couple is married, the more they look like one another? If we marry ourselves purely to God, and are faithful to Him, we see His face and begin to look more and more like Him. What could be better than that? He is "altogether lovely".

Blessed [are] the peacemakers: for they shall be called the children of God.   –Mat 5:9

This speaks of those whose lives actively promote peace. Some people's lives actively promote conflict. They walk into a room and create tension. They are the people who come to family gatherings (or church business meetings) expecting to create a "scene". On the other hand, there are those whose lives promote peace. They are peacemakers. They seek to bring peace and unity among men. They are called the children of God because children behave as their Father behaves. God is the peacemaker; we should strive to be like Him. You might say, "Well, God doesn't know my family", or, "God doesn't know my boss". Oh, yes He does.

The rest of Jesus' teaching here in Matthew, chapter five, deals with the response of the "world" to the believer and our reciprocal behavior. In this world, we can expect ridicule, even persecution, from those who do not understand the face of God. If you "look like" your Father, you can expect the same misunderstanding in your promotion of God's love that His Son endured. Jesus looked like God and the world rejected Him. Jesus teaches us to rejoice and be glad in the midst of this rejection. Be salt and light upon the earth, to season and enlighten those around you. Jesus goes on, in this great sermon, to give some very practical advice regarding Christian lifestyle. While we are not going to explore all of Jesus' words in the rest of Matthew 5 here, we encourage you to study them carefully. Every believer should take time to study Jesus' *Sermon* often.

In the last verse of chapter five, Jesus says, *"Be ye perfect, even as your Father in heaven is perfect".* "Being" is a constant effort. For instance, if I say to my children, *"Be good",* I am speaking that to them because I know it requires ongoing diligence in their striving for goodness. Jesus was not suggesting that we could become absolutely perfect like God while on earth. Indeed, Jesus said that *only God is good.* (Mat. 19:16) This should never, however, be used as an excuse for failure or laziness. Rather, let goodness be a high mark to aspire to. We are made "perfect" and acceptable to God the Father only by the blood of Jesus. Let that blood bring about a *fullness of salvation* in you. Read of the *benefits* of salvation in Psalm 103:

Praise the LORD, O my soul; all my inmost being, praise his holy name. Praise the LORD, O my soul, and forget not all his benefits-who forgives all your sins and heals all your diseases, who redeems your life from the pit and crowns you with love and compassion, who satisfies your desires with good things so that your youth is renewed like the eagle's. The LORD works righteousness and justice for all the oppressed. He made known his ways to Moses, his deeds to the people of Israel: The LORD is compassionate and gracious, slow to anger, abounding in love. He will not always accuse, nor will he harbor his anger forever; he does not treat us as our sins deserve or repay us according to our iniquities. For as high as the heavens are above the earth, so great is his love for those who fear him; as far as the east is from the west, so far has he removed our transgressions from us. As a father has compassion on his children, so the LORD has compassion on those who fear him; for he knows how we are formed, he remembers that we are dust. As for man, his days are like grass, he flourishes like a flower of the field; the wind blows over it and it is gone, and its place remembers it no more. But from everlasting to everlasting the LORD's love is with those who fear him, and his righteousness with their children's children-with those who keep his covenant and remember to obey his precepts. The LORD has established his throne in heaven, and his kingdom rules over all. Praise the LORD, you his angels, you mighty ones who do his bidding, who obey his word. Praise the LORD, all his heavenly hosts, you his servants who do his will. Praise the LORD, all his works everywhere in his dominion. Praise the LORD, O my soul. -Psalm 103:1-22 NIV

The Heart Is A Multiplier   Chapter Two

The heart of man multiplies whatever enters it.

Here in the famous parable of the sower, Jesus speaks of seed and soil:

A sower went out to sow his seed. And as he sowed, some fell by the wayside; and it was trampled down, and the birds of the air devoured it. Some fell on rock; and as soon as it sprang up, it withered away because it lacked moisture. And some fell among thorns, and the thorns sprang up with it and choked it. But others fell on good ground, sprang up, and yielded a crop a hundredfold. When He had said these things He cried, He who has ears to hear, let him hear! Then His disciples asked Him, saying, What does this parable mean? And He said, To you it has been given to know the mysteries of the kingdom of God, but to the rest it is given in parables, that seeing they may not see, and hearing they may not understand. Now the parable is this: The seed is the word of God. Those by the wayside are the ones who hear; then the devil comes and takes away the word out of their hearts, lest they should believe and be saved. But the ones on the rock are those who, when they hear, receive the word with joy; and these have no root, who believe for a while and in time of temptation fall away. Now the ones that fell among thorns are those who, when they have heard, go out and are choked with cares, riches, and pleasures of life, and bring no fruit to maturity. But the ones that fell on the good ground are those who, having heard the word with a noble and good heart, keep it and bear fruit with patience. –Luke 8: 4-15 NKJV

A believer seeking to know their place in the Kingdom must understand this principle: **the heart is a multiplier**.

The Greek for heart is *kardia*, the soul or mind, as it is *the fountain and seat of the thoughts, passions, desires, appetites, affections, purposes, and endeavors.*

The heart sometimes symbolizes the spirit and sometimes the soul. Of course, it is neither but is used to represent either at various times. The Jews believed the heart contained the emotions. We still refer to the heart that way. For instance, we say "I love you with all my heart". We use the heart to represent our emotion and passion. We wouldn't say, "I love you with all my liver". It just isn't romantic! Notice how closely the Greek word for soul or mind, *kardia*, is to our English word, *cardiac*, which means "having to do with the heart". We learn in the English dictionary that *cadiac is* derived from the Greek word, *kardia*, which refers to *both the physical heart and the soul (mind)*.

Whatever is fully received into the heart will multiply. See the young man who takes his first drink. **If that "seed" takes root**, he may develop a lust for alcohol. He may develop a physical or emotional (fleshly) dependency as that seed takes root. We may see him twenty years later as he struggles against the ravages of alcoholism. See him another twenty years later as he lies on his deathbed with liver disease. This morbid illustration is a common life scenario. What has happened? The seed of lust (emotional passion) for alcohol was placed in this young man in a situation which may have seemed innocent enough to him. The heart has taken that seed and multiplied it many times over to bring ruin to this life as his body has cooperated with his soul. Worry can produce death, too. Let's say a young person has a tendency to worry about circumstances of life. It may be easily handled in their youth but the seeds of worry begin to take root and grow in their heart. It becomes anxiety and depression and may lead to larger problems, sometimes even suicide as their body cooperates with the soul. Satan knows and attempts to use in a perverse way the principle of heart multiplication. The perversion of heart multiplication, seducing you to allow self-destructive, unbalanced emotions and lusts into your heart, is a tool Satan uses to promote his goal. That goal is to rob you of God's purpose, power and peace.

Jesus said the *cares of this world and the deceitfulness of riches* can choke out the Word of God in our heart. What begins as one or two thorns can become a briar patch, multiplied by the heart (the soul). Did you ever have a little problem (a small seed) that you began to dwell on and before long, you were thinking of every negative scenario possible. Your mind became consumed with the negative potential and a mole hill became a mountain. Your heart has multiplied the negative many times over. This is why God tells us to think on good things. God's Word is good. When His Word is planted in our heart, and received fully, it takes root and is multiplied.

Finally, brothers, whatever is true, whatever is noble, whatever is right, whatever is pure, whatever is lovely, whatever is admirable —if anything is excellent or praiseworthy—think about such things. *–Phil. 4:8 NIV*

How can the soil of your heart be more fertile and pure? It has to do with the way you respond to the struggles of life, what Jesus called *the cares of this world and the deceitfulness of riches.* Those struggles, trials, tests and temptations must become an integral part of your victory. Every trial, every temptation is to be conquered with the help of Jesus and becomes compost for the soil. The soil of your life is richer every time you crucify (deny) your flesh (body + soul) and, thereby, win another battle over the flesh. Spirit grows stronger and more dominant, allowing the seed of the Word of God to multiply in you. Here is a very simple example: suppose a person is convicted to lose weight. They pass the pie counter and coconut pie calls out to their flesh. There may be a physical and emotional craving for that delicious pie! That is *resistance*; you might call it the deceitfulness of riches in that it appears as earthly richness to their soul. Indeed, it is! Now, they can compromise and satisfy that longing of their flesh but they violate the conviction of God in their spirit. They give their soul and body dominance, dominion in their life. Or, they can pass up the pie and crucify flesh, giving spirit dominion by obeying the Word of God. What will happen to the flesh which was craving that pie? That part of their flesh which would have fed on the pie will die and become compost for the soil of their life. The seed of the Word becomes more deeply rooted in good, rich, fertile soil. *Your* "pie" may be drugs, alcohol, sex, fame, wealth, or many other deceitful riches. On the other hand, you may struggle with cares of this world. Worry, illness, doubt, fear, relationships, finances, self-esteem, insecurity, and more. Those areas of resistance must be faced and conquered too, with the help of Jesus, so that they not choke out the seed. Victory over any struggle can become compost to enrich the soil. Religion, too, can choke out the seed. Some people's "rocky soil" is their quest for religion. They are satisfied only as long as the latest flash of "revival" emotion lasts. Your walk must be by faith, not emotion or sight. Excessive emotion, even in religion, is the dominance of soul over spirit. Spirit dominance is trust in God and any emotional blessing is just that, a blessing, not a foundation. Some people can also develop rocky religious soil when they become obsessed with one doctrine and it grows disproportionately to the Word of God as a whole, choking out the fullness God intends.

Your life will become defined by your struggles or by your overcoming spirit.

Struggle comes into every life. No exceptions. Some lives become defined by struggles. Struggles take root and choke out the seed of the Word. Many people talk about the effects of certain struggles for a lifetime. They love to tell the story of their old struggle and its effects on their life. It has taken root. They wallow still in the "glory" of the struggle, yes even defeat, they faced twenty years ago. Their life, dominated by emotion of the soul, has become dominated by that struggle or those struggles. The Word can not properly root in that heart. It is impossible. The soil is poor and there is little room for the roots, let alone fruit from the seed. In a life defined by an overcoming spirit, only victory over the struggle is retained and the struggle itself is compost. Let your life be defined by victory in Christ.

Even failure can be turned into triumph. Sometimes, we must live overcoming lives in the midst of ongoing challenge. For instance, Paul asked three times that a thorn be removed but God sovereignly left the thorn. But God promised that His (God's) grace would be sufficient even in the midst of the struggle.

And we know that all things work together for good to them that love God, to them who are the called according to [His] purpose.
–Romans 8:28

We like the way Matthew records Jesus' words in verses 22 and 23 of the Parable of the Sower:

Now he who received seed among the thorns is he who hears the word, and the cares of this world and the deceitfulness of riches choke the word, and he becomes unfruitful. But he who received seed on the good ground is he who hears the word and understands it, who indeed bears fruit and produces: some a hundredfold, some sixty, some thirty. - Mat 13:22-23 NKJV

Jesus said our heart has the potential to take the Word of God (the seed) and multiply it thirty-fold, sixty-fold and one-hundred-fold. Now, wouldn't you prefer to be that kind of believer? Don't you want the soil of your heart to be enriched by the Holy Spirit to multiply the Word in you so you become a 100-fold producer, knowing your place of fruitfulness in the Kingdom! Those are the believers who do great exploits to the glory of God. As great as their ministries have been, what if Billy Graham, David Wilkerson, James Robison, Oral Roberts, Kenneth Hagin, Kenneth Copeland, Charles Capps, Joyce Meyers, Beth Moore, T. D. Jakes, James Dobson, Don Wildmon, Josh McDowell, Adrian Rogers, Rick Warren, D. James Kennedy and other great contemporary men and women of God are *30 or 60-fold producers* in the Kingdom! What if there are still untapped treasures of Kingdom fruit to be harvested by the manifested sons of God? What if the 100-fold producers are *yet to come* and that is why you hunger and thirst after the Kingdom of God and His righteousness! You may think "That is ridiculous! How could I be a 100-fold producer"? Well, maybe the Apostle Paul was one of a handful of 100-fold producers to whom we could point. What was he before he was an apostle? Before he was Paul? By his own admission, he was the worst of the worst among sinners. He was a *terrorist*, a *persecutor* of believers. But one day, on the road to Damascus, Jesus supernaturally planted a seed in him and closed his eyes to the world. Jesus said, "Paul, it's hard to kick against the pricks (sharp sticks embedded along the side of the road to keep oxen centered), isn't it?" He was forced to stop kicking against the plan of God for his life. Saul recognized Jesus and obeyed. Shut up in a house on Straight Street, his eyes blind to the cares of the world and the deceitfulness of riches, we do not know what all happened in his heart. But it was significant enough, revelatory enough, that, after Ananias prayed for him, he was filled with the Holy Spirit and awarded his purpose in the Kingdom. It was such a major *transformation* that his name changed! We revere Paul as being, perhaps, one of only a handful of 100-fold producers in the Kingdom. But even Paul didn't get there overnight. Paul speaks often of his struggle against flesh and his quest for spirit dominance, for a more perfect, more mature, more effectual walk with God. Now, if Saul could become Paul, what could you become as the seed multiplies in good soil? A 100-fold producer to the glory of God?

Let's look at another example which is not so positive. See the wealthy young man noted in Luke, chapter 18. He asked Jesus what he had to do to discover his place in the Kingdom. Jesus told him to observe commandments and the young man said he had followed all those commandments from youth! Jesus said, "You lack only one thing. You are rich toward this world. Sell everything and give it to the poor. Then, come back, knowing your treasure is in heaven, and your place in the Kingdom will be as one of my personal disciples. You can walk with Me." But the rich young man who lived what was apparently a "good" life by standard of the law could not crucify that last of flesh and missed his place in the Kingdom. He left with sorrow in his heart. Jesus then tells his disciples that it is easier for a camel to go through the eye of a needle than for a rich man to enter into the Kingdom, finding his purpose and place in the Kingdom. The disciples wonder aloud how **anyone** can find their place in the Kingdom. *They asked "How can **anyone** be saved?"* They and Jesus are speaking of more than salvation unto heaven. They are speaking of salvation unto the perfect plan of God for one's life! Jesus explains that finding ones place in the Kingdom is impossible for man in his flesh but states that *with God, all things are possible*. This is a major clue to life! We can not find purpose, power and peace within our flesh. The Galatian believers, having become followers of Christ, then tried to become mature or perfected in their works. Didn't work. They were called foolish by Paul. We cannot save ourselves and we cannot grow ourselves. Only God, by His Spirit, can work this maturity in us and only then can we find our purpose, God's pleasure, in us.

*And be not conformed to this world: but be ye **transformed** by the renewing of your mind* (this is a work of the Holy Spirit), ***that ye may prove what [is] that good, and acceptable, and perfect will of God [in your life].*** -Romans 12:2

Do you desire the seed, the Word, to be multiplied in you? Do you desire to be a 30, 60 or even 100 fold producer for the Father? Do you desire to know the abundance, maturity, fruition, fullness, completion, perfection, righteousness, peace and joy planned for your life? To accomplish these goals, your life must be balanced. We're not talking about some new-age perversion of Christian doctrine; we're talking about the balance of spirit, soul and body that brought Paul to a place where he said, "*...for I have learned, in whatsoever state I am, to be content."* Paul found a balance of spirit, soul and body, in submission to the Holy Spirit, with his spirit ruling over soul and body in his life. He prayed that other believers would find the same.

And the very God of peace sanctify (perfect) you wholly; **and [I pray God] your whole spirit and soul and body** *(*note the order; it's no mistake!) **be preserved blameless** *unto the coming of our Lord Jesus Christ. — I Thes. 5:23*

Unity With God　　　　　　　Chapter Three

And one of the scribes came, and having heard them reasoning together, and perceiving that he had answered them well, asked him, Which is the first commandment of all? And Jesus answered him, The first of all the commandments [is], **Hear, O Israel; The Lord our God is one Lord: And thou shalt love the Lord thy God with all thy <u>heart</u>, and with all thy <u>soul</u>, and with all thy mind, and with all thy <u>strength</u>** *(spirit, soul and body): this [is] the* **first commandment.** *—Mark 12:28-30*

See, first, that Jesus proclaimed the unity of the Trinity. The phrase, **The Lord our God is one Lord**, when studied in the Greek, indicates unity. Jesus is declaring the unity of the Trinity. Jesus certainly should understand that unity! As a part of the Trinity, He became flesh and dwelled among us. He, the Word, became flesh and is our example. The human part of Jesus had to learn submission of his spirit to the Father and dominance of His spirit over flesh just like we do. See him in the wilderness (Luke 4), before he begins the fullness of his mission, struggling against the temptations of the enemy. The enemy appealed to His flesh and Jesus overcame by the Word of Father God. His spirit was dominant over flesh. He worked in harmony or unity with the Father. We sometimes call this AGREEMENT. In answering the question about the greatest commandment, Jesus declares the necessity of unity toward God in our tri-part being. All three elements of spirit, soul and body are included in the greatest commandment.

Now, what if you can mature to a balance of spirit, soul and body in *your* being? God's creation coming into unity or balance with God, who is the definition of unity in Trinity, results in incredible synergy. *Synergy is a working together in agreement of various elements to bring about effectual power.* The power in the Trinity is the greatest example of synergy! Agreement in the Godhead resulted in creation!

It is no small thing that our tri-part being is to be united in love for God. This love brings unity with God.

The principle of agreement is very large in the Kingdom of God. God chooses to use this principle to bring all things to fullness, completion, maturity in the life of the believer. Our role as believers is to believe the Word of God with all our spirit, soul and body. This is the principle of agreement.

But without faith [it is] impossible to please [him]: for he that cometh to God must believe that he is, and [that] he is a rewarder of them that diligently seek him. -Hebrews 11:6

Then said they unto him, What shall we do, that we might work the works of God? Jesus answered and said unto them, This is the work of God, that ye believe on him whom he hath sent. —John 6: 28-29

Our believing is called FAITH. It is not our ability to accomplish anything within ourselves. Believing or faith is trusting in the faithfulness of God the Father, Jesus the Son, and the Holy Spirit to accomplish our completion. All three members of the Godhead work in *agreement-harmony-unity-perfect oneness* to complete us. It is God's desire that our spirit, soul and body work in harmony within our tri-part being in a similar way and that we work in synergy with Him.

Being confident of this very thing, that He which hath begun a good work in you will perform [it] until the day of Jesus Christ. -Phil 1:6

God the Father, Son and Holy Spirit in unity + your spirit, soul and body in unity = the purpose of God, the power of God, and the peace of God in your life.

This is the picture of the believer who lives out of the dominance of their spirit, being matured in the mind of Christ and having the agape' heart of the Father flowing through them to others.

Rather than being dominated by unbalanced soulish emotion and the flawed reasoning which results, they are alive unto God.

And the very God of peace sanctify you wholly; and [I pray God] your whole spirit and soul and body be preserved blameless unto the coming of our Lord Jesus Christ. Faithful [is] He that calleth you, who also will do [it]. - I Thes. 5: 23-24

Let's observe an example of *spirit dominance*. Look at Caleb:

*But my servant **Caleb**, because he had **another spirit** with him, and hath followed me **fully**, him will I bring into the land whereinto he went; and his seed shall possess it. -Num. 14:24*

*Save **Caleb** the son of Jephunneh the Kenezite, and **Joshua** the son of Nun: for they have **wholly** followed the LORD. -Num. 13:12*

The scripture says Caleb had a "different" spirit. It infers the same about Joshua. He and Joshua believed God's promise while the other ten spies did not. You can read the entire story in Numbers, chapters 13 and 14, if you are not familiar with it.

Caleb and Joshua followed God WHOLLY. They followed God with their whole being; *spirit, soul and body*. There was perfection in their love for and trust in God. There was harmony of spirit, soul and body in their love and faith. That dominance by their spirit in submission to God's Word, with their flesh (soul and body) in agreement in faith, led them to the Promised Land. The other ten knew God's promise but FEAR seized their flesh, stole the seed of promise, and dominated them. They never found their *perfected or matured promise* in the Kingdom because emotion ruled and robbed them.

Many people are seeking purpose; most never find it. The average believer will tell you they feel less than satisfied that they have discovered fullness of purpose in their life. Less than satisfied that they live in the fullness of abundance Jesus promised or that their life produces the power God intended in and through them. If there is ONE KEY to finding purpose in life, it is this: *LOVE GOD with all your heart, soul, mind and strength... your spirit, soul and body.* Perhaps we haven't fully understood what Jesus meant by those words. *Learn to express that love creatively to your Father.* God created man for fellowship, for intimate fellowship with the Godhead. See that David worshipped **from his spirit** and his emotions and body followed as he was very expressive to God in emotional words and physical dance! God Himself said David was a man after His heart! That is the picture of a spirit-dominated man yet we can see times when David let his flesh, his emotions and lusts, rule over him. When that happened, he got in trouble!

God patterned marriage between man and woman after the intimacy **He** desires. Man and woman in unity as one as God originally intended are to have tremendous spiritual power. See God's **original intent** perfectly expressed in the garden as He fellowships intimately with Adam and Eve, walking with them in the garden during the cool of the day. After that order was broken, see in the scriptures all that God has done and does to bring man into restoration of that fellowship. From ordinance of burnt offerings to the sacrifice of His Son, God constantly draws man to Himself. **If you are on a quest for spirit dominance, start here in intimate fellowship with God.** You can read every book, hear every sermon, and order every recording on the subject but none of these things can compare to intimate, personal time with the Father. The Holy Spirit, as you express love for God with your whole being, will be your teacher and bring you into glory after glory (level after level) of purpose in God. You will find God's pleasure in loving Him with all your being in unity. Being ONE in agreement with God brings *purpose, power and peace into the believer's life.* This is fullness. Lay aside this book for a season of worship. Confess your love for God before Him. Worship Him from your spirit. Call your flesh into agreement and love Him for a while. Tell Him you want to love Him more creatively and fully by learning spirit dominance. Ask Him to give you revelation by His Spirit so that you might please Him, finding your purpose in the Kingdom more perfectly. God responds to that kind of love. Try it! **You will find spirit dominance only by loving God in spirit and in truth.**

But the hour cometh, and now is, when the true worshippers shall worship the Father <u>in spirit and in truth</u>: for the Father seeketh such to worship Him. God [is] a Spirit: and **they that worship Him must worship [Him] in spirit and in truth.** *-John 4: 23-24*

Sometimes believers struggle to express their love for God, to know their love for God adequately, because they don't understand how much God loves them. They feel unworthy of his love as indeed we all are. But God's love for us is not based on our worthiness. **God is not limited in His love for us by His flesh because He doesn't have any flesh!** We sometimes struggle to love others because our negative emotions or reasonings are involved. **God doesn't filter His love for you through negative reasonings and emotions regarding His knowledge of you. God is SPIRIT. God is LOVE.** He loves us by His grace. Remember, grace is *the merciful kindness by which Jesus gives you His favor, exerting His holiness upon you, that you might increase in the faith, knowledge and affection of the Father.* How do you know God loves you? God did the biggest thing He could do when He gave His only Son Jesus to die for you, to pay the price for your sins. Some people say, I wish God would do this or that so I could see His love for me. No. God already did the biggest thing He could do. What greater love is there than the sacrifice of a child? An only child! God did that for you even though you don't deserve it. That's why it's called grace. Grace is undeserved favor.

Surely he took up our infirmities and carried our sorrows, yet we considered him stricken by God, smitten by him, and afflicted. But he was pierced for our transgressions, he was crushed for our iniquities; the punishment that brought us peace was upon him, and by his wounds we are healed. We all, like sheep, have gone astray, each of us has turned to his own way; and the

LORD has laid on him the iniquity of us all. He was oppressed and afflicted, yet he did not open his mouth; he was led like a lamb to the slaughter, and as a sheep before her shearers is silent, so he did not open his mouth. By oppression and judgment he was taken away. And who can speak of his descendants? For he was cut off from the land of the living; for the transgression of my people he was stricken. He was assigned a grave with the wicked, and with the rich in his death, though he had done no violence, nor was any deceit in his mouth. Yet it was the LORD's will to crush him and cause him to suffer, and though the LORD makes [c] his life a guilt offering, he will see his offspring and prolong his days, and the will of the LORD will prosper in his hand. After the suffering of his soul, he will see the light of life and be satisfied; by his knowledge my righteous servant will justify many, and he will bear their iniquities. Therefore I will give him a portion among the great, and he will divide the spoils with the strong, because he poured out his life unto death, and was numbered with the transgressors. For he bore the sin of many, and made intercession for the transgressors. -Is. 53: 4-12 NIV

That's how much God loves you. You don't feel that lovable? We're not suggesting for a moment that you are, that any of us are. Doesn't that make our God all the more wonderful and lovable, that He, by His character of grace, loves us in our present condition and works in us to make us more into His own image? By loving us when we are unlovable, He then brings us to a place of maturity in Him where we become more lovable! God is the Father who knows the potential of his child. **You are a diamond in the rough, but you are a *completed diamond in God's eyes of faith*. You are a shapeless lump of clay, but you are a *beautiful vessel in God's eyes of faith*.**

For whom he did foreknow, he also did predestinate [to be] conformed to the image of his Son, that he might be the firstborn among many brethren. Moreover whom he did predestinate, them he also called: and whom he called, them he also justified: and whom he justified, them he also glorified. What shall we then

say to these things? If God [be] for us, who [can be] against us? **He that spared not his own Son, but delivered him up for us all, how shall he not with him also freely give us all things?**
--Romans 8: 29-32

God is a very generous Father, desiring to *freely give you all things*. "All things" means *every blessing of life necessary for you to live out the fullness of God's purpose and pleasure in you.* God intends for believers to look like Jesus who looks like the Father. In other words, God intends for you to look like Him, your Father. God has a plan, a *predestination, a good and perfect plan,* for everyone who believes. That does *not* release you from personal responsibility. You must *cooperate* with that predestination. Everyone reading this book has a potential place of great value in the Kingdom. Every person on earth has **opportunity to believe on Jesus and mature into the fullness of God's plan in their life. You must believe.**

Why do most people miss this fullness? Because they live out of their flesh. They are dominated by their souls which includes unbalanced emotions and reasonings. After all, it isn't *logical* to the average person to believe and fully trust in God. And even if your emotions lead you to God, they won't keep you there. They lead you to the next valley in the roller coaster called life! Up and down, in and out of your purpose.

How depressing? NO! Our purpose is to lead you *out of depression* to a place of understanding, even revelation by the Spirit. Be transformed by the renewing of your mind and know the perfect will of God in your life, your place in the Kingdom (Romans 12:2). Transformation does not usually happen overnight for most believers. It is a process. That is the way Peter described *grace and peace multiplied (II Peter 1), a process.* You don't interrupt a process until a product is complete. You don't go into the garden and pick a tomato until the plant is matured and the tomato is ready for harvest! **Sometimes on your journey, you will feel like you are on a roller coaster even as you seek spirit dominance. Flesh** dies hard. You will be disappointed in yourself at times as you struggle in your flesh. Don't give up. Don't get under condemnation. Ask the Holy Spirit to help you on your journey and He will.

And the Word was made flesh, and dwelt among us, (and we beheld His glory, the glory as of the only begotten of the Father,) full of grace and truth. John 1: 14

Jesus was the **WORD of God** born to earth. He reflected the glory of God and manifested the Kingdom of God. We are to be a work of the Word worked in us by the Holy Spirit to bring us to maturity. We, like Jesus, are to be the reflection of the glory of God, manifesting His Kingdom upon the earth. God's grace and revelation of truth in us is to grow from level to level. Paul called it glory to glory.

But we all, with open face beholding as in a glass the glory of the Lord, are changed into the same image from glory to glory, [even] as by the Spirit of the Lord. - 2 Cor. 3:18

The Word tells us, in Romans 12: 2, not to conform to the world but to be transformed by the renewing of our mind. Renewal of mind is more than the inputting of knowledge. **It is the revelation of knowledge, that is, the Holy Spirit revealing truth (God's Word), in you and maturing you progressively.** Paul realized that knowledge alone would not complete us, that the love of God would be necessary to bring fullness. He prayed that we might be able...*to comprehend with all saints what [is] the breadth, and length, and depth, and height; And to know the love of Christ, which passeth knowledge, that ye might be filled with all the fullness of God. -Eph. 3: 18-19*

Every time God stretches us or grows us in faith, He does it for our growth in His love.

As we renew our minds in the Word, the Holy Spirit begins to show us mindsets, attitudes, and sin in our lives. **But until we**

allow the Word to become established deep in our spirit, we will not be transformed. How many believers know the Word in their soul (their mind) but their lives are not transformed by that knowledge? **You can have a truth deep in soul but shallow in spirit.** Testing comes to challenge knowledge and draw it from the soul into the spirit.

My brethren, count it all joy when ye fall into divers temptations; Knowing [this], that the trying of your faith worketh patience. But let patience have [her] perfect work, that ye may be perfect and entire, wanting nothing. James 1: 2-4

We must come to embrace the testing of our faith because it produces patience. This is NOT patience as we think of it, but KINGDOM PATIENCE which is very active and progressive. We think of patience as passive; Kingdom patience is *alive* in us to work completion. **It is this Kingdom patience which must have her perfect work that we might be complete, lacking nothing. James is referring to balance of spirit, soul and body, with spirit dominant.** It is in Kingdom patience that we learn to abandon ourselves to God, not leaning unto our own understanding and not allowing the testing circumstances to bring *unbelief*. **Too many believers never come into fullness because when testing comes, they fear, doubt, refuse, rebel or abort, not allowing patience to have her "perfect work".** When knowledge of truth has gone through the testing of fire, it becomes established in your spirit, making your spirit more dominant. Flesh dies in the fire of testing, and balance is achieved. As God's grace is poured into the believer, it encourages the fruit of the Spirit, the character of God.

I have been crucified with Christ and I no longer live, but Christ lives in me. The life I live in the body, I live by faith in the Son of God, who loved me and gave himself for me. - Gal. 2:20 NIV

Isn't the whole seed and soil concept, as Jesus told it, a process? And isn't there resistance along the way of process? Don't those seeds have to burst forth into roots, and don't those roots have to press deep into soil before they find their purpose, producing good fruit? And don't those fruit look like their "father fruit" when finished? An apple seed is to go through the process of producing an apple tree and ultimately produces an apple, which looks like the parent apple which produced the little seed which was placed in the soil! But it doesn't happen overnight. It is a process, a lifelong process of being matured, perfected, sanctified in His love. We must embrace the JOY of testing.

Count It All Joy   Chapter Four

My brethren, **count it all joy when ye fall into divers temptations**; *Knowing [this], that the trying of your faith worketh patience. But let patience have [her] perfect work, that ye may be perfect and entire, wanting nothing.* –James 1:2-4

We like both the King James and NIV versions here. To assure clear understanding, let's include the NIV text of this same verse:

Consider it pure joy, my brothers, whenever you face trials of many kinds, because you know that the testing of your faith develops perseverance. Perseverance must finish its work so that you may be mature and complete, not lacking anything. –James 1:2-4 NIV

Considering struggles to be a joy goes against the flesh. Your soul and body will naturally moan and groan about struggles. Struggles can be defined by a multitude of temptations and challenges, not just temptation to sin. Any struggle can be a testing of your faith. Struggles come into every life. Every life, without exception. And they will come no matter how much you groan and moan or resist them. Perhaps your struggle is a physical illness or limitation. Maybe your challenge is relational, emotional or financial. Your struggle may include the *cares of the world and the deceitfulness of riches* as Jesus describes them in the parable of the sower. Or they may be the conviction of the Holy Spirit to DO SOMETHING in obedience to God. Sometimes our flesh doesn't want to obey! There is an understatement!

Struggles of any kind are intended *by the enemy* to choke out the Word within you and to stunt your growth. Remember, Satan's desire is to rob, kill and destroy God's purpose in us. **Struggles are intended *by the Father* to grow you into a mature believer, to lead you into the fullness of your place**

in the Kingdom, to develop you into a child of God who looks like his or her Father! Your response to your struggles makes the difference. You are to count struggles as JOY. Your life will be defined by your struggles or by your joyous, overcoming spirit. When you face your struggles with the joy of the Lord, which scripture describes as your strength *(Nehemiah 8:10)*, that joy acknowledges the trying of your faith as working patience (endurance and steadfastness) in you. Our joy grows as do all things in the Spirit. We face the testing of our faith and learn to deal with the struggles by the spirit, not our soul. We experience the joy of the Lord (our strength) as we learn to see the promise of God "afar off" by faith. Faith (believing in God's faithfulness) forces soul and body into their proper order under spirit. When you comprehend that the only way you are going to move forward in the things of God is to have your faith tested, you may learn to embrace the testing of your faith with joy. Only by faith do we come to fullness or completion, becoming partakers of the divine nature, the character, of the Father.

When you face the trials of life, be encouraged by God's promise:

No weapon forged against you will prevail, and you will refute every tongue that accuses you. This is the heritage of the servants of the LORD, and this is their vindication from me," declares the LORD. —Is. 54:17 NIV

Understand this; **faith and patience** are married. So are **abandon and trust. You must believe in the faithfulness of God, faithfully and patiently abandoning your flesh unto God, trusting in God to complete you**. If we don't learn to embrace the testing of our faith (our trust and belief in God), we can not profit as God desires. The **embracing of our testing is our cooperation with the Holy Spirit** in our lives. Testing stretches and grows us in His love. Every time God allows the stretching of our faith, He is growing us in His love. Count it joy!

It is our **perseverance of faith** (that simply means we believe wholly in God's Word) which overcomes flesh, strengthens our spirit, and takes us to the glory of spirit dominance.

If you exercise faith, patience, abandon and trust toward God, patience will have her perfect work, making you complete, lacking nothing. Perhaps there is no greater battle than this. Our flesh wants to whine when we face challenges. It is one of the strongest tendencies of our fleshly nature. Your flesh will fight you on this one, but if you will *in your spirit, by the help of the Holy Spirit*, demand that your flesh come into agreement with your spirit in JOY, you will make great advances in finding your place in the Kingdom. Even as your flesh whines, rejoice in your spirit during times of challenge or resistance. You rejoice by believing God's Word as truth over your challenge. You live by faith, believing the Word of God to be bigger than your struggle. Literally call for your soul and body, your flesh, to come into agreement with the joy of the Lord in you. Place your spirit in a position of dominance over your soul and body.

Rejoice evermore. Pray without ceasing. In every thing give thanks: for this is the will of God in Christ Jesus concerning you. Quench not the Spirit. Despise not prophesyings. Prove all things; hold fast that which is good. Abstain from all appearance of evil. **And the very God of peace sanctify (perfect or mature) you wholly; and [I pray God] your whole spirit and soul and body be preserved blameless** *unto the coming of our Lord Jesus Christ.* **Faithful [is] He that calleth you, who also will do it.** *- I Th 5: 16-24*

The theme of seed and soil continues in James when he speaks specifically of temptation to sin.

But every man is tempted, when he is drawn away of his own lust, and enticed. Then when lust hath conceived, it bringeth forth sin: and sin, when it is finished, bringeth forth death. –James 1: 14-15

Even believers sometimes have errant thoughts. Sometimes your mind will present lustful thoughts to you which will make you blush! Do not allow those seeds to take root; take them captive and make them obedient to the Word of God. Do not allow them to come into agreement with Satan. If they conceive, becoming pregnant, they bring forth sin which can ultimately lead to death. This does not necessarily refer to physical death, though it can. Illegal drug use, for instance, may lead to a weakened mind and body, your mind and body being robbed or "dying". It can also lead to death. The spirit also suffers weakness in this situation, being robbed of its full potential in Christ. "Death" may refer to the death of the fullness of God's purpose in you.

Satan desires to rob you. God wants you to know His fullness. Look at Paul's words to the Ephesians:

This I say therefore, and testify in the Lord, that ye henceforth walk not as other Gentiles walk, in the vanity of their mind (human reasonings and emotions), *having the understanding darkened, being alienated from the life of God through the ignorance that is in them, because of the blindness of their heart* (their soul, that is, their reasonings and emotions): *Who being past feeling* (insensitivity to their spirit-unable to feel conviction) *have given themselves over unto lasciviousness* (a mindset which can't get enough sin), *to work all uncleanness with greediness. But ye have not so learned Christ; If so be that ye have heard Him, and have been taught by Him, as the truth is in Jesus: That ye put off concerning the former conversation the old man, which is corrupt according to the deceitful lusts; and be renewed in the spirit of your mind; and that ye put on the new man, which after God is created in righteousness and true holiness. —Eph. 4:17-24*

James (chapter 1) describes the Father as one who gives freely to His children as we trust in Him. He describes the Father as the giver of *every good gift* as we trust Him. God's Word, the seed described by Jesus in the parable of the sower, works His pleasure, His ordained purpose, in us. James refers to the sower and seed concept again when he calls God's Word, *the engrafted Word.*

For the wrath of man worketh not the righteousness of God. Wherefore lay apart all filthiness and superfluity of naughtiness, and **receive with meekness the engrafted Word, which is able to save your souls***. But be ye doers of the Word, and not hearers only, deceiving your own selves. For if any be a hearer of the Word, and not a doer, he is like unto a man beholding his natural face in a glass: For he beholdeth himself, and goeth his way, and straightway forgetteth what manner of man he was. But whoso looketh into the* **perfect law of liberty, and continueth [therein]**, *he being not a forgetful hearer, but a doer of the work, this man shall be* **blessed in his deed.** *-James 1: 20-25*

Then said they unto Him, What shall we do, that we might work the works of God? Jesus answered and said unto them, **This is the work of God, that ye believe on Him whom He hath sent.** *—John 6: 28-29*

The *wrath of man which* **James refers to is man's natural, fleshly character.** Moaning and groaning in the face of adversity. **Wanting to run, give up or abort the test.** Do you *hear* the Word of God regarding facing adversity with joy? You can be a hearer and not a doer and you profit nothing. You miss the fullness of your place in the Kingdom by not persevering. **But, if you are a doer and you press into the JOY of adversity, patience does her work, making you more complete or perfect in the image of the Father. You and the Kingdom of God profit**. Meditate on that. Read James 1: 20-25 in full again. Open your Bible and read all of James 1; it is powerful!

James said you can look in a mirror, see yourself, and quickly forget what you look like. Try this; think what your best friend looks like. You have no problem seeing that image in your mind's eye, right? Now, *see your image* in your mind's eye. Not so easy. Just as you can look into a mirror, look away and quickly forget what you look like, you also can hear God's Word and quickly forget it, being only a hearer, not a doer. But if you see **the Word of God, His plan, the perfect law of liberty, and continue in it**, you become a person *"blessed in his deed"*. **Your deed is *your making*, according to the Greek. In other words, the person who actually does what the word says, counting resistance as JOY, will be blessed in the process of discovering their purpose, their being completed.**

If we don't grow in our faith and learn to embrace the testing of our faith, the *stretching* of our faith by God, we can not grow from glory to glory (level to level). **We can only become spirit dominant and overcome the dominance of emotions, reasonings and lusts by growing in faith, *trusting God's promise, what James calls the "perfect law of liberty".***

Paul refers to this *law of liberty* in II Corinthians, chapter 3.

Now the Lord is that Spirit: and where the Spirit of the Lord [is], there [is] liberty. But we all, with open face beholding as in a glass the glory of the Lord, are changed into the same image from glory to glory, [even] as by the Spirit of the Lord. - II Cor. 3: 17-18

So much is revealed in this scripture. As we just read, James used the illustration of looking into a mirror or glass and seeing self. Paul uses the illustration here of looking into the perfect law of liberty, *the glory of the Lord*, and being changed into that same image from glory to glory (level to level). **Simply put, this means that as we continually look into the mirror of the Word, we become more like that image. The Word is Jesus; the Word became flesh and dwelt among us.** Therefore, we look into the Word, the face of Jesus, and see the reflection of God's glory in the face of Jesus Christ.

For God, who commanded the light to shine out of darkness, hath shined in our hearts, to [give us] the light of the knowledge of the glory of God in the face of Jesus Christ. - II Cor. 4: 6

As we look into the Word of God, we become increasingly like that image of God, reflecting the glory of God as Jesus did. From *glory to glory* indicates a lifelong process of perfecting or maturing. When we come to the end of life on earth, we should still be looking into the perfect law of liberty, still being transformed progressively into the image of God. Our death ushers us into the presence of God where that transformation is **absolute**. Wouldn't you like to be a 30, 60 or 100-fold producer upon the earth before your *absolute* completion in heaven?

Both Jesus' parable of the sower and James' exhortations indicate that the cares of this world and the deceitfulness of riches, our fleshly desires, must be crucified that the seed of God may grow in us. James, by inspiration of the Holy Spirit, tells us how. **COUNT IT ALL JOY!**

Now unto Him that is able to do **exceeding abundantly above** *all that we ask or think, according to the* **power that worketh in us** *[the Word of God], Unto Him [be] glory in the church by Christ Jesus throughout all ages, world without end. Amen.*
–Ephesians 3: 20-21

Paul In The Process   Chapter Five

If Paul, formerly Saul, the persecutor of believers, can make it through the process, surely you can too. Even though he had a life-transforming, spirit-regenerating experience on the road to Damascus, Paul still had to go through the process of sanctification, maturing or being perfected in his Kingdom purpose. And what resistance he faced! Maybe he was one of the few 100-fold producers in history! A seed was planted on the road to Damascus. It had to grow in Paul just like it does in us. And sometimes, that is a struggle. There are struggles **from without,** like when Paul was being stoned or jailed. And there are struggles **from within,** like when Paul was facing internal conflict. Here are his words:

I do not understand what I do. For what I want to do I do not do, but what I hate I do. And if I do what I do not want to do, I agree that the law is good. As it is, it is no longer I myself who do it, but it is sin living in me. I know that nothing good lives in me, that is, in my sinful nature. For I have the desire to do what is good, but I cannot carry it out. For what I do is not the good I want to do; no, the evil I do not want to do—this I keep on doing. Now if I do what I do not want to do, it is no longer I who do it, but it is sin living in me that does it. So I find this law at work: When I want to do good, evil is right there with me. For in my inner being I delight in God's law; but I see another law at work in the members of my body, waging war against the law of my mind and making me a prisoner of the law of sin at work within my members. What a wretched man I am! Who will rescue me from this body of death? Thanks be to God—through Jesus Christ our Lord! So then, I myself in my mind am a slave to God's law, but in the sinful nature a slave to the law of sin. –Rom. 7: 15-25 NIV

Paul faced the classic struggle between flesh (soul and body) and spirit. But he persevered in the faith and won! And he explained to us how we can win too. Paul says there are two laws at work which bring the conflict between our flesh (our soul and body working together for domination of our life) and our spirit. One is the *law of sin and death*; the other is the *law of liberty*. It may help you to remember the verse in which Jesus says of His disciples, **The spirit is willing but the flesh is weak (Mat. 26:41).** This indicates that there is, for the believer, the task of overcoming flesh **by the spirit. If flesh dominates, it will be manifested in *incompletion* or lack of fullness of purpose in our life. If spirit dominates, flesh will come into agreement for fullness of purpose.**

The law of sin and death in our flesh struggles against the Word in us to choke it out, to hinder our process of completion. C. S. Lewis said "No man knows how bad he is until he tries to be good". Some say Paul must surely have been describing his life ***before*** his salvation. Why? Don't you, as a believer, face the same struggle? Don't we all! **This is Paul, <u>as a believer</u>, walking through the process of maturity.** This is Paul realizing there is a battle for his soul. The law of death wants to capture his soul and rule his life. This is Paul patiently growing into his place in the Kingdom. Paul cries out in his weakness, declaring himself to be wretched. He sees the moral bankruptcy of self. We all must see this bankruptcy of self and fall on the mercies of God in Christ.

What a wretched man I am! Who will rescue me from this body of death? Thanks be to God—through Jesus Christ our Lord! So then, I myself in my mind am a slave to God's law (another way of saying, "the spirit is willing"), but in the sinful nature a slave to the law of sin (another way of saying, "the flesh is weak"). —Romans 7: 24-25 NIV

Deliverance from the *law of death in the flesh* unto the *law of liberty in the spirit* is accomplished only in Christ our Lord. There is no other way. It is *not of works, lest any man should boast.*

For by grace are ye saved through faith; and that not of yourselves: [it is] the gift of God: Not of works, lest any man should boast. For we are his workmanship, created in Christ Jesus unto good works, which God hath before ordained that we should walk in them. –Eph. 2:8-10

When the word "saved" is used, we often think simply of salvation from hell. But being *saved* is much more than that. Being *saved* is being rescued from hell and delivered unto eternal life with God all right, but it is also *a keeping unto your purpose, the plan and pleasure of God for your life on earth.* It is the sum of all benefits which accrue to the believer as a result of the grace of God through Christ His Son, through the blood of Jesus. This was worked in Paul and is worked in us in the same way; it is worked by grace through faith. Whose faith (faithfulness)? His and yours. Your faithfulness is to believe His Word, that He is God and able to save by grace manifested in Christ. That *He is absolutely faithful* to keep His Word.

Through faith also Sara herself received strength to conceive seed, and was delivered of a child when she was past age, **because she judged Him faithful who had promised. -Hebrews 11:11**

Your faithfulness is believing in Him. His faithfulness is that *He keeps* His promise in response to your believing! Like Sara, you must judge Him faithful!

[There is] therefore now no condemnation to them which are in Christ Jesus, [who walk not after the flesh, but after the Spirit]. **For the law of the Spirit of life in Christ Jesus hath made me free from the law of sin and death. For what the law could not do, in that it was weak through the flesh, God sending His own Son in the likeness of sinful flesh, and for sin, condemned sin in the flesh: That the righteousness of the law might be fulfilled in us, who walk not after the flesh, but after the Spirit.** *For they that are after the flesh do mind the things of the flesh; but they that are after the Spirit the things of*

the Spirit. For to be carnally minded [is] death; but **to be spiritually minded [is] life and peace***. -Romans 8: 1-6*

Only Jesus gives freedom. Because the blood of Jesus was required to *set us free*, **we must understand it is required to keep us free.** And, according to verses 38 and 39 of the same chapter, it does a very good job of keeping us free! Nothing can separate us from the love of God which is in Christ Jesus our Lord.

Realizing we must walk after the Spirit, we bring pleasure to God and His purpose to our life. Study all of Romans 8 and see that it is true. The law of sin and death no longer condemns us for we are set free, ruled by the law of liberty in Christ. We are advanced in the maturity of our freedom in Christ.

But whoso looketh into the perfect law of liberty, **and continueth [therein]***, he being not a forgetful hearer, but a* **doer of the work***, this man shall be blessed in his* **deed***. -James 1:25*

Remember, **your deed is your making**, **the unfolding of God's Word in you by the Holy Spirit.** And that *making* comes by cooperating with the Holy Spirit, believing the promise of God in your life. True faith is always manifested in your active obedience to God's Word. After all, James said, *"Faith without works (obedient acts) is dead (James 2:17)".* Mature love for God is manifested in obedience. Jesus said, "If you love Me, you obey Me (John 14:15)."

Then said they unto Him, **What shall we do, that we might work the works of God?** *Jesus answered and said unto them,* **This is the work of God, that ye believe on Him whom He hath sent.** *–John 6: 28-29*

Walking after the Spirit is being a doer of the work by **continuing in the law of liberty**. If you walk outside the spirit, following your flesh, you will not please God and you will not find the fullness of your purpose in the Kingdom. We're not saying you are not saved or that you won't go into God's presence if you die. If you sincerely believe on Jesus for your salvation, even if you never follow a path to maturity, you are on your way to heaven. Most believers never find fullness but they are still saved. **But don't you want to go into God's presence as a 30, 60 or even 100-fold producer in the Kingdom! Don't you want the fullness of your salvation?**

Perfected Love   **Chapter Six**

There is a doctrine called *perfected love*. You rarely see it mentioned by this name. Some people refer to perfected love as *sanctification*. It is the process of your cooperation with the Holy Spirit to work the power of God's Word in you to develop holiness. John Wesley taught this doctrine and was unjustly criticized for it, being misunderstood. The common misunderstanding about this doctrine is the perception that it proposes that a believer can be **absolutely** free from sin. We are not proposing a doctrine of *sinless perfection*. Certainly, the believer who is in the process of being perfected in love can sin, but *not while he is walking in that perfected love.* Here's how John Wesley put it:

*In this peace (*the process of sanctification- love being perfected*) they remain for days or weeks, or months... and commonly suppose they shall not know war anymore; till some of their old enemies, their bosom sins, of the sin which did most easily beset them, (perhaps anger or desire) assault them again, and thrust sore at them, that they may fall. Then arises fear, that they shall not endure till the end; and often doubt, whether God has forgotten them, or whether they did not deceive themselves in thinking their sins were forgiven. Under these clouds, especially if they reason with the devil, they go mourning all day long. But it is seldom long before their Lord answers for Himself, sending them the Holy Ghost to comfort them, to bear witness continually with their spirits that they are the children of God.* -John Wesley

Now, let us examine some scripture regarding freedom from sin:

This then is the message which we have heard of Him, and declare unto you, that God is light, and in Him is no darkness at all. If we say that we have fellowship with Him, and walk in darkness, we lie, and do not the truth: But if we walk in the light, as He is in the light, we have fellowship one with another, and

the blood of Jesus Christ his Son **cleanseth us from all sin**.
- I John 1: 5 - 7

*My dear children, **I write this to you so that you will not sin. But if anybody does sin**, we have one who speaks to the Father in our defense—Jesus Christ, the Righteous One. He is the atoning sacrifice for our sins, and not only for ours but also for[a] the sins of the whole world. We know that we have come to know him if we obey his commands. The man who says, "I know him," but does not do what he commands is a liar, and the truth is not in him. But if anyone obeys his word, **God's love is truly made complete in him.** This is how we know we are in him: Whoever claims to live in him must walk as Jesus did.*
-I John 2: 1-6

There seems to be a conflict, even within these verses. We are told we are **cleansed from all sin** and, then, we are told that *if we sin*, we have an advocate with the Father, that advocate being the Son, Jesus Christ. Actually, the two statements are in perfect harmony. **We are cleansed from all sin-sins of the past and sins of the future. All sin.** That doesn't mean we will never sin after we are saved but that all sin past, present and future is covered or cleansed by the blood of Jesus. That should motivate us, not to sin, but to abstain from sin in gratitude and in search of matured love.

What shall we say, then? Shall we go on sinning so that grace may increase? By no means! We died to sin; how can we live in it any longer? Or don't you know that all of us who were baptized into Christ Jesus were baptized into his death? We were therefore buried with him through baptism into death in order that, just as Christ was raised from the dead through the glory of the Father, we too may live a new life. If we have been united with him like this in his death, we will certainly also be united with him in his resurrection. For we know that our old self was crucified with him so that the body of sin might be done away with, that we should no longer be slaves to sin—because anyone who has died has been freed from sin. Now if we died with

Christ, we believe that we will also live with him. For we know that since Christ was raised from the dead, he cannot die again; death no longer has mastery over him. The death he died, he died to sin once for all; but the life he lives, he lives to God. In the same way, count yourselves dead to sin but alive to God in Christ Jesus. Therefore do not let sin reign in your mortal body so that you obey its evil desires. Do not offer the parts of your body to sin, as instruments of wickedness, but rather offer yourselves to God, as those who have been brought from death to life; and offer the parts of your body to him as instruments of righteousness. For sin shall not be your master, because you are not under law, but under grace. What then? Shall we sin because we are not under law but under grace? By no means! Don't you know that when you offer yourselves to someone to obey him as slaves, you are slaves to the one whom you obey— whether you are slaves to sin, which leads to death, or to obedience, which leads to righteousness? But thanks be to God that, though you used to be slaves to sin, you wholeheartedly obeyed the form of teaching to which you were entrusted. You have been set free from sin and have become slaves to righteousness. -Romans 6: 1-18 NIV

Sin does not *reign and rule* in the life of a believer. Love is to be perfected toward God. Your spirit is to be dominant over your flesh. But, we are told that *if we sin* (indicating it is possible), we have an advocate with the Father in Jesus. The most awesome believers I have known still sin on occasion when they follow their flesh for a moment or for a season. The danger in teaching **absolute** perfection on earth is that the believer embracing such a doctrine will invariably find himself terribly disappointed, even alienating himself from fellowship with God, when he fails (sins). We are going to sin during seasons when we begin to listen to our flesh rather than our spirit. When we give soul and body (emotions, reasonings, cravings) dominant place in our life, getting out of balance or agreement, we will sin. When we walk after the spirit, we will not. **The key to freedom from sin is to become progressively and aggressively passionate in our love for God, loving Him with our whole heart, soul, mind**

and strength. When our love is in this place of "perfection", we do not sin. How can one who loves completely offend the one they love? A person who completely and passionately loves their spouse will not commit adultery. One who loves God passionately and completely will not commit adultery toward God. Jesus said, "If you love Me, you will obey Me." Indeed, when we are walking in that love, we will not sin. **Why would we even desire sin when we are dominated by our spirit in submission to the Word?**

This is HOLINESS. Holiness is a topic which draws much contention and disagreement. There is no need for such. I Peter 1:16, quotes God, "Be ye holy, for I am holy". In other words, my kids ought to look like Me! Read forward a few verses and holiness is explained. It is manifested in our love for God and one another! Holiness is God's presence. In man, it is His presence manifested in us. We usually define holiness by what someone does NOT do. *He doesn't commit adultery, swear, drink or chew so he must be holy.* When you look at God's holiness, do you look at the fact that God doesn't commit adultery, swear, drink or chew? No, you look at his love. Ephesians 5 tells us to be *imitators of God, walking in love*! God is set apart from the unholy unto holiness because of His love, not legalism. Holiness is His love perfected in you. When Jesus was asked about the greatest commandment, He did not answer with what we would commonly call a "holiness" commandment! He answered with two "love" commandments. You see, holiness will grow out of love but love can not grow out of holiness because there is no holiness without love. Which came first, holiness or love? Love. A believer desiring holiness in his or her life should be taught love, not holiness. Those believers who have found love perfected will live holy lives. It is in this place that we find victory over the sins which easily beset us.

The commandments, "Do not commit adultery," "Do not murder," "Do not steal," "Do not covet," and whatever other commandment there may be, are summed up in this one rule: "Love your neighbor as yourself." Love does no harm to its

neighbor. Therefore love is the fulfillment of the law.
–Rom 13:9-10 NIV

There it is! Holiness, being set apart from sin, is lived out by love! Your motivation for refusing sin is your love for God and for others!

When you are in that place of walking after the spirit, you don't sin because you love God too much and that love is center-stage in your life. And you love your fellow man too, loving your neighbor as yourself. It is when your mind wanders from that love, from God's presence, and begins to embrace self-centered desire that you sin. That's why believers are to take every thought captive.

Casting down imaginations, and every high thing that exalteth itself against the knowledge of God, and bringing into captivity every thought to the obedience of Christ.   -II Cor. 10:5

Wherefore seeing we also are compassed about with so great a cloud of witnesses, let us lay aside every weight, and the sin which doth so easily beset [us], and let us run with patience the race that is set before us.   -Hebrews 12:1

It is an amazing thing about the nature of man that he can move in and out of God-centeredness and self-centeredness so often, like a roller coaster. While a believer may drift toward selfish desire from time to time, and even dwell there for a short season, he will not remain there or allow that selfish desire to reign in him. For instance, an adulterer is defined as *one who practices adultery as a way of life and he will not enter the Kingdom.* A believer who has slipped into an adulterous relationship but has truly repented and does not practice that way of life routinely has momentarily fallen *from the perfection of love for God but not from grace! His sins are forgiven.* A person who has **given themselves over to adultery** will not enter the Kingdom of God. One who has failed by following a selfish desire for such immoral relationship but has repented and returned to his first love in

Christ is forgiven. The same can be said of other sin-gossip, for example. The one who falls into the sin of gossiping has fallen from the *perfection* of God but not from the *grace* of God. If they repent, their sins are forgiven.

How much better to *remain* in that love for God, to be progressively perfected in it and achieve victory over the flesh!

If anyone acknowledges that Jesus is the Son of God, God lives in him and he in God. And so we know and rely on the love God has for us. God is love. Whoever lives in love lives in God, and God in him. In this way, love is made complete among us so that we will have confidence on the day of judgment, because in this world we are like Him. There is no fear in love. But perfect love drives out fear, because fear has to do with punishment. The one who fears is not made perfect in love. We love because he first loved us. If anyone says, "I love God," yet hates his brother, he is a liar. For anyone who does not love his brother, whom he has seen, cannot love God, whom he has not seen. And he has given us this command: Whoever loves God must also love his brother. - 1 John 4: 15-21 NIV

But if ye be led of the Spirit, ye are not under the law. Now the works of the flesh are manifest, which are [these]; Adultery, fornication, uncleanness, lasciviousness, Idolatry, witchcraft, hatred, variance, emulations, wrath, strife, seditions, heresies, Envyings, murders, drunkenness, revellings, and such like: of the which I tell you before, as I have also told [you] in time past, that they which do such things shall not inherit the kingdom of God. But the **fruit of the Spirit is love, joy, peace, longsuffering, gentleness, goodness, faith, meekness, temperance**: *against such there is no law. And they that are Christ's have crucified the flesh with the affections and lusts. If we live in the Spirit, let us also walk in the Spirit. Let us not be desirous of vain glory, provoking one another, envying one another. -Gal. 5: 18-26*

Pure love, the love of God, is the most powerful force in the universe. It is a purifying force. The believer perfected in love is purified from pride, from lustful desire and self-will, from fear, from doubt, from insecurity, from guilt, shame and condemnation.

There is no fear in love; but perfect love casteth out fear: because fear hath torment. He that feareth is not made perfect in love. - I John 4:18

For God hath not given us the spirit of fear; but of power, and of love, and of a sound mind. - II Tim 1:17

Love never fails. It is supreme. All the character of God emanates from His heart of agape' (love). All of His compassion and all of His judgement emanate from His agape'. As wonderful as prophecies, tongues and knowledge may be, they will fail, cease and vanish away. Love will remain.

(9)For we know in part, and we prophesy in part. (10) But when that which is perfect is come, then that which is in part shall be done away. (11) When I was a child, I spake as a child, I understood as a child, I thought as a child: but when I became a man, I put away childish things. (12) For now we see through a glass, darkly; but then face to face: now I know in part; but then shall I know even as also I am known. (13) And now abideth faith, hope, charity, these three; but the greatest of these [is] charity (love).-1Cor.13:9-13

That which is perfect has sometimes been interpreted as referring to the Second Coming of Christ and *that which is in part* has been interpreted as prophecies, tongues and knowledge. But look more closely. Verse 10 must be read as a bridge between 9 and 11 to understand the proper context. Paul is speaking of *knowing in part* in verse 9. In other words, he is speaking of a believer not yet matured. The first phrase of verse 10 speaks of the arrival of maturity, sanctification, pefected love. When maturity comes, immaturity leaves. Then, in verse 11, he reinforces that thought. In verse 12, Paul says when we are immature, we see the truths of the Kingdom dimly. When we become matured by the process of our love being perfected by the Spirit, we see Kingdom things more clearly as if we are face to face with God. We finally see God clearly as He sees us! And faith, hope and love reign in us.

Paul is speaking of the love of God perfected in the believer. Unfortunately, most have interpreted this passage as indicating a maturity which occurs *after we die*, in heaven. This causes the believer to set his sights low and miss the mark. God intends that we have life more abundantly in Jesus on the earth. You can know a level of God's agape', seeing His face more clearly, through a process of maturation worked by the Spirit of God. **God has given us the "Promised Land" but we have to walk in the Spirit to get there**. God will work this perfection in our human spirit by *the Holy Spirit*. This is a perfection which will never be arrogant and puffed up. It is a righteous, not self-righteous, perfection. Perfect love can not exist in anything less than the soil of a humble heart.

Perhaps we will not know the **absolute** fullness of this love until we reach heaven, but it is God's intention that we be growing in His love from glory to glory, level to level, while we live out our faith journey on earth!

Go After The Process   Chapter Seven

*For the word of God [is] quick, and powerful, and sharper than any twoedged sword, piercing even to the **dividing asunder of soul and spirit, and of the joints and marrow**, and [is] a discerner of the thoughts and intents of the heart. –Heb. 4:12*

We have spoken of the perfecting or maturing of our love as a process. Here, the Word of God is described as a *worker of the process* of dividing spirit, soul and body into proper relationship. The believer is, therefore, made more complete or perfect in their journey.

Most people avoid processes. Process involves change, and people don't like change. They get in their comfort zones and don't want to budge. David, on the other hand, prayed, "I will run the way of Thy commandments, when thou shalt **enlarge my heart**.". (Ps. 119:32) David, *who was far from a sinless man*, was nonetheless, a man after God's heart. He prayed to know God's ways, for his heart to be enlarged so he might contain the heart of God. Finding your place in the Kingdom is not so much about your *ability* as much as it is about your *expandability*. There are lots of pretty religious bottles but very few fresh wineskins. A fresh wineskin is somewhat like a balloon. Take a 16 ounce, plastic bottle and an uninflated round balloon. Compare them side by side. Most people would choose to contain their fullness in the bottle. It's very tangible and safe. Fill it up, put the cap on, and forget it. The balloon, on the other hand, is a little vulnerable and stretchy! It expands to hold more and more and will hold 32 ounces! Will you choose to hold your fullness, your purpose, your blessing in a 16 ounce bottle or in a balloon? We must desire fresh wineskins, pliable and well-oiled by our obedience to the Word and by our desire for the working of that Word by the Spirit in us, ready to expand, ready to contain the mysteries of God's heart. **Going after your purpose, your fullness in the Kingdom is not a simple thing. It requires**

violent, diligent, aggressive pursuit of the heart of God, His Kingdom.

And from the days of John the Baptist until now the kingdom of heaven suffereth violence, and the violent take it by force. - Mat. 11:12

The violent are those who forcefully seek the truth and pleasures of the Kingdom. You must go after the Kingdom. If you aggressively, forcefully seek the Kingdom, you will receive it. That's the promise of God. Does that not imply that the spiritually lazy will not receive fullness?

How do you forcefully take the Kingdom?

By aggressively and progressively loving God will all your spirit, soul and body.

Jesus said *all the law and the prophets* hang on that one principle of love for God. As your love for God grows, the Kingdom will grow in you. You will be an instrument of His will upon the earth. You become the answer to the Lord's model prayer. You also become the answer to the prayer Jesus prayed just before He left this earth.

They are not of the world, even as I am not of it. Sanctify them by the truth; your word is truth. As you sent me into the world, I have sent them into the world. For them I sanctify myself, that they too may be truly sanctified. My prayer is not for them alone. I pray also for those who will believe in me through their message, that all of them may be one, Father, just as you are in me and I am in you. May they also be in us so that the world may believe that you have sent me. I have given them the glory that you gave me, that they may be one as we are one: I in them and you in me. May they be brought to complete unity to let the world know that you sent me and have loved them even as you have loved me. Father, I want those you have given me to be with me where I am, and to see my glory, the glory you have given me because you loved me before the creation of the world.

Righteous Father, though the world does not know you, I know you, and they know that you have sent me. I have made you known to them, and will continue to make you known in order that the love you have for me may be in them and that I myself may be in them.   -John 17:16-26 NIV

We are to be one with the Godhead. We are to be one in ourselves, in harmony in spirit, soul and body. We are to be one with one another as believers. When we are, we find our place in the Kingdom. In a way, we bring His Kingdom upon the earth. Non-believers come to believe through our unity. To know this unity, you will have to aggressively seek the Kingdom of God. The Kingdom of God in you, the Word as seed made mature, will result in your living out your purpose in the Kingdom while still upon the earth. **You live on earth but your citizenship is in heaven. You progressively receive revelation of God's mysteries. Earthly fact becomes eclipsed by Kingdom Truth**. For example, a financial struggle comes. That is *fact*. Kingdom Truth says God will meet all my needs according to His riches in glory by Christ Jesus (Phil. 4:19). Your doctor says you have a disease. He speaks *earthly fact* according to knowledge. **Kingdom Truth** says that by the stripes which were applied to Jesus, you are healed (I Peter 2:24). **Kingdom Truth** says the prayer of faith will heal the sick (James 5:15). What worry, struggle or lustful desire is NOT dealt with by God's Word? None. Every care of this world, every deceitfulness of riches is answered by God's Word. His Word, deeply rooted in you, which is His Kingdom come in you, brings you into **Kingdom Truth** and releases you from the corruption of earthly fact. Would you rather live by earthly fact or Kingdom Truth? Automatically, someone will answer, "Why, Kingdom Truth, of course!" The truth is **a person ruled and dominated by their flesh will prefer earthly fact**. Have you ever been around believers who reveled in their illnesses? They can't wait to tell you about their latest trip to the doctor. Some people enjoy their illness so much, they don't want healing. Or regarding offenses, they celebrate their conflicts and wallow in self-pity. Some people, even believers, choose earthly fact over Kingdom Truth.

But the mature believer, ruled by a spirit submitted to God's Word, embraces KINGDOM TRUTH. In KINGDOM TRUTH, you are more than a conqueror in Christ Jesus! Haven't you met believers who were chronically ill with a severe disease who, even in their illness, reflect a full measure of God's love and character? Those are people who have embraced Kingdom Truth and they trust God's grace in the midst of their struggle while they wait for healing.

Some believers do not revel in their struggle; they abhor it. But they do not know how to overcome fully. A life illustration from Gary: My father was a tremendous man of God, a preacher, mostly a pastor, for 60 years. I am confident my father would approve of my sharing this insight into his personal life if it helped only one person; that is the kind of generous man he was. Dad suffered from chronic depression and abnormal anxiety. I remember several times that my father became so emotional about simple conflicts in the church that he wound up in the emergency room with his heart racing, fearing death. And such anxiety in a man who was normally strong in the faith. A most beloved pastor. But Dad never found complete peace because he never had revelation of spirit dominance. Cares of the world choked out fullness of the seed planted in him. At about age 50, I began to experience increased, abnormal anxiety. I decided to go to my doctor, an excellent physician. I explained my dad's history of depression and anxiety and how I was feeling. The diagnosis was "general anxiety disorder". "In your father's day", my doctor said, "the drugs used to treat this were heavy and addicting with undesirable side-effects so your father probably avoided them. Now we have medications which treat this effectively and safely. Here's a prescription; take these and in two weeks or so, you should feel much better."

That's great! I was excited to hear of such a simple cure. I took the medicine home and showed my wife. She asked, "Are you going to take that?" How dare her challenge my faith! Then, I called my co-author and prayer partner. Excitedly, I told her what my doctor said and that I had the cure! She said "Are you going to take that?" Checked in my spirit by my wife and my friend, I fell on my face before God that night and cried out for guidance. The Spirit whispered this impression to my heart....*your doctor's diagnosis is correct. On earth, your struggle is called general anxiety disorder. That is fact. Here in the Kingdom, we call it fear. You can take the medicine which is mercy or you can stand on Kingdom Truth and be healed. Both are good and are gifts from God. Kingdom Truth is superior.* I asked my wife to pray. I asked Pam to pray. I never took one pill. I chose Kingdom Truth. I have never experienced another day of abnormal anxiety. I have been tempted but I have never experienced another day of abnormal anxiety. Praise God for His faithfulness.

Don't get me wrong. I revere my dad as one of the most powerful men of God I have ever known. He was the ultimate pastor. He loved God and loved His people. He mentored other pastors. He substantially found His purpose. He was a great husband to my mom and a great father. But as high as his level of perfected love was, he still lived substantially out of his soul at times, led by his emotions in some areas, and he suffered for it. He never knew spirit dominance fully in his life. He was a 30, maybe even a 60-fold producer in the Kingdom! That's awesome! What if he had known a greater revelation of Kingdom Truth and could have been set free from anxiety and depression? He would have been even more free to follow his purpose. My father knew God had given us a spirit of power, love and a sound mind. I cannot explain why he did not more violently go after it. I think he probably went after it at the level of revelation he knew. Paul said we go from glory to glory, looking more like our Heavenly Father, as we stare into His face. But the great apostle Paul, himself, may have died with some area (described as a thorn) still incomplete. He had to lean on the sufficiency of God's grace with regard to that thorn. There are ways in which I wish I looked more like my earthly dad. He had some of the glories of the Heavenly Father that I don't have.

There are ways in which I am glad I don't look like my dad; I am glad to be free of anxiety and depression and wish he (and his mother and his grandmother) could have been. **I will strive, with revelation regarding balance of spirit, soul and body, the spirit being dominant, to look more like my *heavenly* Father. That's what my earthly father would want for me. I wish I had been able to share the revelation in this book with Dad. He would have embraced it fully.**

We want to say a word about medicine, including anti-depressants. All good gifts are from God. Anti-depressants may be **God's mercy** gift to you. Do not use the testimony here as an excuse to quit your medications *of any kind*. Many believers take anti-depressants and lead fuller and more effectual lives thanks to the mercy of medicine. Work with your doctor if you decide to believe for healing. Do not suddenly stop your medication. It is not wisdom. God gives the gift of mercy through medicine, surgery and other therapies to bring healing to some. Do not despise it but rejoice in it until you find a greater glory. The same God who gives healing also gives wisdom and mercy.

You will know the Kingdom of God in fullness only as you seek it violently with persistent faith. Blind Bartemeus would still have been blind if he hadn't made himself vulnerable to the crowd's criticism along the road and yelled out to Jesus. The woman with the incurable illness would not have been healed if she had not pressed through the resistance of the crowd. Zaccheus would not have found salvation if he had not climbed a tree to get above the crowd. The man on the stretcher would never have walked if his friends had not come into agreement to press through the crowd and tear the roof off the house! You may have to receive criticism, cry out, press through the crowd, and "tear off a roof" to find fullness in the Kingdom. But in every case, it is worth it. Loving God aggressively is worth it. Believing violently is worth it.

A life illustration from Pam: I was near the fullness of a work of spiritual healing in my life when my daughter, Jennifer, was born. I had prayed diligently for a little girl to love. In the beginning of her life, I could love and care for her with my entire heart. But as her personality began to develop, I saw things in my daughter that I did not like. She was very headstrong and clashed with me on everything. If I called something white, she called it black. Whatever clothes I picked out for her, she either disliked or pretended to dislike. She became very hard to handle emotionally and I did not like her. I remember one night when Jennifer was about 5 years old, I told the Lord I did not know if I loved my own daughter. God spoke to my heart and told me that if I were obedient, my rejection of Jennifer could be broken. He impressed me that I would love my daughter and have relationship with her unlike anything I could imagine. So began a walk of faith, patience, abandonment and trust unlike anything I had ever known.

The Holy Spirit would often urge me to express love to my daughter in various ways when everything in me wanted anything but closeness with Jennifer. I would obey, calling my flesh into submission, but I still didn't *feel* love for my daughter. Some days were better than others and there were many times I cried out to God for forgiveness because I felt like a failure. On one of the nights when I cried out in despair, God revealed to me that victory is not in the *perfection* of obedience. It is in the *willingness* to obey because you believe God's Word. During this journey of obedience, a transformation took place as flesh died in me and the Holy Spirit did a supernatural work in me. The love of God began to flow freely from my spirit and the acts formerly done in obedience became my joyful desire. The hugs that I had forced myself to give in obedience became the very desire of my heart. The pure love of God flowed from my heart to Jennifer. I became free to love my daughter and a spirit of rejection was broken. This journey took about eight years to complete. For eight years, I had to embrace this process though there was little sense of the time until I looked back in reflection. I had to live out faith, patience, abandonment and trust for the full season of

God's unfolding grace. Because I was willing to believe His Word and walk in obedience by faith, I now have an awesome relationship with my daughter. We are best friends.

Grace And Peace Multiplied   Chapter Eight

Peter, by the Holy Spirit, wrote some of the most awesome words about being perfected and finding your place in the Kingdom. How many times have we all read these words without revelation? Let these words come alive in you.

Grace and peace be multiplied to you in the knowledge of God and of Jesus our Lord, as His divine power has given to us all things that pertain to life and godliness, through the knowledge of Him who called us by glory and virtue, by which have been given to us exceedingly great and precious promises, that through these you may be partakers of the divine nature, having escaped the corruption that is in the world through lust. But also for this very reason, giving all diligence, add to your faith virtue, to virtue knowledge, to knowledge self-control, to self-control perseverance, to perseverance godliness, to godliness brotherly kindness, and to brotherly kindness love. For if these things are yours and abound, you will be neither barren nor unfruitful in the knowledge of our Lord Jesus Christ. For he who lacks these things is shortsighted, even to blindness, and has forgotten that he was cleansed from his old sins. Therefore, brethren, be even more diligent to make your call and election sure, for if you do these things you will never stumble; for so an entrance will be supplied to you abundantly into the everlasting kingdom of our Lord and Savior Jesus Christ.   -2 Peter 1:2-11 NKJV

Peter is clearly writing to believers. **Grace** is the quality of God's character which favors the undeserving believer and promotes him toward fullness in Christ. It encourages, strengthens and nourishes our faith, pressing us toward personal unity with the character of God. Peter prays that it is multiplied in you. **Peace** is the assurance, the confidence of our position in Christ, which comes by the working of grace. **Peter prays for grace and peace multiplied.** Grace, then peace. He couples them because he knows grace multiplied will bring peace multiplied.

He goes on to explain how they grow. Grace and peace are multiplied in the believer by a more precise and full understanding (knowledge) of God's promise. Peter says in verse three that God has, by His divine power, given us knowledge which leads us to His glory and virtue (His excellence of character-righteousness). As a matter of fact, according to Peter, God has issued knowledge which leads to fullness of life and reverence for God. Verse four indicates that all this is done with purpose. After all, God never speaks an idle Word!

.... by which have been given to us exceedingly great and precious promises, that through these you may be partakers of the divine nature, having escaped the corruption that is in the world through lust -2 Peter 1:4 NKJV

The knowledge, the great and precious promises which God gives by His divine power, is given for the purpose of bringing us into unity with God's divine nature, making us partakers of His divine Nature, His character. Free from the corruption (death) upon the earth. Now, that's spirit dominance! Our spirit linked with God to exhibit His character. To bring His Kingdom upon the earth! To do His will! A partaker is a *partner, associate or companion*. Grace and peace are to promote us, by God's promises, toward partnership, agreement, unity with God's nature. Shall we just dwell here for a moment and let this sink in? How can it get any better than that!

Then, Peter lists God's character traits and urges us to grow in them.

But also for this very reason, giving all diligence, add to your faith virtue, to virtue knowledge, to knowledge self-control, to self-control perseverance, to perseverance godliness, to godliness brotherly kindness, and to brotherly kindness love. -2 Peter 1:5-7 NKJV

Peter is praying that believers grow in grace and peace, becoming partakers in agreement with God's character. God desires, promotes and provides for partnership with you, that His nature becomes your nature! Why?

For if these things are yours and abound, you will be neither barren nor unfruitful in the knowledge of our Lord Jesus Christ. For he who lacks these things is shortsighted, even to blindness, and has forgotten that he was cleansed from his old sins.
-2 Peter 1:8-9 NKJV

Why? Because God wants you to be fruitful in the Kingdom which happens as these things abound in you. The Greek word for "abound" means that the character of God is **existing and increasing in you.** You are being perfected in His love. We are back to that word, "process"! We're back to the parable of the seed and soil! As God's character is abounding (rooting and growing) in you, you are fertile and fruitful in Christ, remembering that He saved you from your sins. Now hear this! Here is the dynamic promise to those in whom grace and peace are multiplied. Here is the Word of God to those who become partakers of the divine nature. Do you want multiplied grace and peace? Do you want spirit dominance? Do you want to know your place in the Kingdom? Your purpose in life?

Therefore, brethren, be even more diligent to make your call and election sure, for if you do these things you will never stumble;
-2Pe 1:10 NKJV

May we paraphrase verse ten? *If you will take Peter's prescription from the preceding verses and stand on it, if you will diligently and violently pursue God's character, your calling and election (the place God has ordained for you) is assured, and you will not falter in your quest for purpose. You will not fall.*

The Greek word for "fall" here means *stumble, fall into misery and become wretched.* We will let the theologians argue over whether this means losing your salvation or never knowing fullness of salvation. *We suggest avoiding either one!* Here's the verse we are anxious, no, make that *excited*, to present:

*For so an **entrance** shall be ministered unto you abundantly into the everlasting kingdom of our Lord and Saviour Jesus Christ.*
-2Pe 1:11 NKJV

As you become partakers of God's divine Nature and abound in His character, a gate swings wide open. After all, you are a partner, an associate, and your personal entrance into the Kingdom of our Lord Jesus is discovered. Traditionally, believers have considered this to mean their *homegoing*. They do all this and then go to heaven. That's not a bad interpretation of this scripture and it's comforting, to be sure. But we think the church should revisit this scripture. We believe Peter is saying that you will find your purpose or place in Kingdom even as you live on this earth. The Greek word for Kingdom here means *of the royal power and dignity conferred on Christians in the Messiah's kingdom*. We believe it is perfectly consistent with the intent of this scripture to express it this way:

If you are aggressively and progressively a partaker in His divine Nature, the gate to your position and purpose in the Kingdom of God will swing wide open. You aggressively and progressively become a joint heir with Jesus. You look more and more like your Father. You fulfill God's purpose for your life…right here, right now! Is this the place Paul had found when he said, "I have learned to be content in all things"? A place of fully trusting God to work "all things together for good"? A place of "in everything give thanks for this is the will of God in Christ Jesus"?

What Would Jesus Do? Chapter Nine

Why would you have less access to the mysteries of the Kingdom of Heaven and produce a less fruitful life than what has been ordained for you when:

1. Jesus Himself said you would do *these works and greater!*

2. As a joint heir, you **share the same Father as Jesus!**

3. You receive the **same Spirit that Jesus did!**

4. You have been given the **keys to the Kingdom!**

5. You have access to the **same resources that Jesus had in heaven!**

6 You have been given the **power of agreement**!

Most of the church has been content to settle for a church experience. Some are pressing forward into Kingdom life. Just as Jesus told the disciples in Matthew 13:11, *only some are chosen to know the mysteries of the Kingdom.* The "chosen" are those who will come into agreement with God, becoming partakers of his divine Nature. You must be interested in Kingdom experience if you are still reading this book! **Here's the greatest mystery of the Kingdom: God loves us! God partners with us! We "deliver" His Kingdom upon the earth!**

Then he called his twelve disciples together, and gave them power and authority over all devils, and to cure diseases.
-Luke 9:1

This is the power that moves mountains and brings life from death. This is the power that calls things that are not as though they are. This is the power that heals the sick and sets the captive free. This is the place of great creativity in promoting the

Kingdom of God on earth. Believers who are primarily and consistently led by their flesh cannot know this power. This power is reserved for those who, by the help of and in cooperation with the Holy Spirit, have crucified flesh and given rule to their spirit in submission to the Word of God.

The balance of this chapter comes as a word of knowledge:

Love never fails. This means that love is never without power. See I Cor 13 again and realize that all things mentioned here may be done without love, being powerless and without profit. Gifts are fraudulent without love. Why waste the faith and power to move a mountain if you have no agape' as your motivation? Will you use mountain-moving faith as a thing of personal profit or pleasure? Or will you use mountain-moving faith in harmony with love to profit others and the Kingdom? To pleasure the heart of God. I Cor 13 is communicating that gifts cannot be expressed *in the Spirit* without love. Though you have the power to do this or that and have not love, it *profits nothing. It is not in the Spirit.* **Therefore, the Father withholds the maturity of certain gifts until love is matured.** The Lord says, *Why would I bestow the gift of healing fully if love is not matured?* Some use the unmatured *seed* of the gift of healing as a toy and even for personal profit in their immaturity. *But when love is mature,* **all glory will be to God and healing gifts will be magnified.** Some use mountain-moving faith as a thing of personal pleasure, a thing to impress the flesh of man. This is immature and without profit. Say to the mountain "be removed and be cast into the sea" but *if this profits only the mover's flesh, there is no profit in the Kingdom or pleasure to the heart of God.*

There is no profit; the same words are used in Galatians. There is no profit in self-righteous "perfection".

It is for freedom that Christ has set us free. Stand firm, then, and do not let yourselves be burdened again by a yoke of slavery. Mark my words! I, Paul, tell you that if you let yourselves be circumcised, Christ will be of no value to you at all. Again I declare to every man who lets himself be circumcised that he is obligated to obey the whole law. You who are trying to be justified by law have been alienated from Christ; you have fallen away from grace. But by faith we eagerly await **through the Spirit** *the righteousness for which we hope. For in Christ Jesus neither circumcision nor uncircumcision has any value. The only thing that counts is faith expressing itself through love. You were running a good race. Who cut in on you and kept you from obeying the truth? That kind of persuasion does not come from the one who calls you. . –Galatians 5:1-8 NIV*

See it is THROUGH THE SPIRIT that perfection comes. In and by or through the Spirit, you wait (the Greek word means *aggressively and confidently anticipate*) for the hope (that is Jesus; only in Him is there hope) of righteousness (the only condition in which man is acceptable to God, having the maturity and character of God). Does this scripture not bear out that you must, in and by the Spirit, aggressively anticipate maturing in Christ? There is no other way. It is through matured relationship, knowing the love of God expressed in the Trinity, that you become effectual in the Kingdom. The hope of righteousness is awaited by faith, both in the confidence you have that Jesus is Messiah and by the faithfulness OF the Messiah. It is not just your faith (remember you have none outside God) but the faith or faithfulness of the Messiah. **You wait on His faithfulness by confidence given by the Holy Spirit. Jesus, the hope of righteousness, is matured in you through the Spirit. The whole process is** *in and by the Spirit and never by self-effort.* *Note that self-righteousness is without profit but faith worketh by love.*

Faith, hope and love remain, says Paul, but the dominant or root of these is love. In Galatians, chapter five, **Paul makes clear that love is the root of everything**. Faith and hope are spoken of here but love is clearly dominant.

FAITH WORKETH BY LOVE. This indicates that the faithfulness of Christ was energized by the love of God.

Your faith will be energized by the love of God. Faith energized maturely by love is ultimate faith.

Observe every truly effectual ministry and see that its root is love. Observe those whom you have admired as genuine and effectual in ministry. See that the root of their ministry was or is love for others. There are HUGE machines that mimic ministry and claim spiritual profit which are without worth in the Kingdom and without pleasure in the Father's heart. See the parades of man-glorifying testimonies. Even when your God works in mercy to touch the infirmed in these situations, it brings little pleasure to His heart as glory is spent or wasted upon man.

Faith worketh by love. *Faith is energized by love.*

If perfected love is your high calling, and it IS, then what must bring effectual and true faith and hope? What must bring profitable tongues, prophecies and the moving of mountains? Here is the completion of the book. Now, it can be finished:

Jesus walked in perfected love. This is the reason He healed effectually. He turned no emotional cartwheels. He did not have to exhibit a show for *His love* **drew men to Him. If He be lifted up, all men will be drawn to Him.**

If you walk in perfected love, men, women and children will be drawn to you without resistance. You will be irresistible as He is irresistible. See that one who experiences your love tells another of your love. This is perfected love, lifting up Jesus and drawing men to Jesus in you.

You were running a good race. Who cut in on you and kept you from obeying the truth? -Galatians 5:7 NIV

See in Galatians 5, verse 7, that many run well but are hindered in their perfection by disobedience. **As you walk in obedience, you are perfected in your love, matured in your love.**

I can point you to men and women who have a level of perfected love but I can point you to none who have reached absolute perfected love. Those with highly perfected love will do the works of Jesus and greater. This is why the Lord dwells on revelation of agape' in you.

Much teaching has been *about* love but without full *revelation of love*. It is necessary to know the receiving and giving of the Father's agape' love. **The maturing of this grace is absolutely essential to your being able to walk in fullness in the Spirit.** Now and in the future, love will be the dominant theme of revelation. All which will be revealed will point to the maturing of your love. Profit comes only through love. Perfected love casts out all fear (doubt) and leaves only confidence. How can you lay hands on the sick and see them recover? The confidence of love. How can you set the captives free and see many come to know Christ? Love. How can you deliver many from the snares of the devil, breaking strongholds and crushing serpents [demonic powers]? Love. How can you comfort those who lack and their loss has overwhelmed? Love. How can you lead those called and chosen to new levels of glory? Love. How can you teach and preach with anointing and clarity? Love. How can you appropriate all the resources of the Kingdom of God? Love. How can you multiply the provisions of earth to be used to My [God's] glory? Love.

Love never fails. In all else, there is failure. Love perfected never fails.

Why has spirit dominance been taught so forcefully and consistently to you? Because only in dominance of the spirit can love flourish and be perfected. What of bodily [physical] love? Can it not become perverted? What of soulish love? Does it not follow error? Only the spirit can comprehend love and command the harmony of the flesh. God is Spirit and communicates love in spirit. *Your flesh will always reach to perversion of truth. Your spirit will always reach to pure love and, when dominant, will rule* *your being in love.* **This is man perfected as the Creator intends, a man dominated by spirit in the love of God.**

Now, look back upon everything. See it in the light of love. Do you not see all more clearly now? Do you see God more clearly, face to face? Rejoice for who has seen God? Surely no man has fully seen God. This means that no man has reached the perfection of love except Jesus. Some have seen more clearly than others but no man hath seen His face most clearly. Rejoice and STAY IN THE SPIRIT. This is the path to the hope of righteousness. This is the path to perfected love. This is the path to His face.

The Pleasures Of God Chapter Ten

By faith Moses, when he was come to years, refused to be called the son of Pharaoh's daughter; **Choosing rather to suffer affliction with the people of God, than to enjoy the pleasures of sin for a season**; *Esteeming the reproach of Christ greater riches than the treasures in Egypt: for he had respect unto the recompense of the reward. -Hebrews 11:24-26*

Moses knew that the ultimate pleasure or reward of God was more pleasant and sweet than the pleasure of sin for a season. **While the pleasure of sin is for a season, the pleasures of God are forevermore.** They are eternal. They are righteousness, peace and joy in the Holy Ghost!

If they **obey and serve [him]**, *they shall spend their days in prosperity, and their years in* **pleasures**. *-Job 36:11*

Thou wilt shew me the path of life: in thy presence [is] fulness of joy; at thy right hand [there are] **pleasures** *for evermore. -Psa 16:11*

They shall be abundantly satisfied with the fatness of thy house; and thou shalt make them drink of the river of thy **pleasures**. *-Psa 36:8*

The Hebrew word for *pleasures* in the first two verses above means *sweetness or pleasantness, satisfaction.* The word for *pleasures* in Ps. 38:8 is *eden*. It means *delight or luxury.* It also means *Eden as in Garden of Eden.* It is restored to those who put their trust in God.

How excellent [is] thy lovingkindness, O God! therefore the children of men put their trust under the shadow of thy wings. -Ps. 36:7

Eden was closed when man broke agreement with God. But through faith in God through Christ, the pleasures of Eden and more are restored to your life. You eat to your satisfaction from the fatness (abundance) of God's house. You are **part of God's household** and you can walk right into the dining room any time you choose and enjoy a meal from his table to your satisfaction! Your drink? You drink from the river of His pleasure, from the river which flows through Eden! *Do you get revelation of that?* You drink from the Eden River, **the river of originally intended fellowship with God.** Eden means *paradise*. God put a river in Eden. What does a water source do for a garden? The Eden River makes your life lush and full.

You have a rich inheritance as a child of God. Need we remind you that God is Jehovah Jireh, *the Lord will provide*? Abraham was obedient, about to offer His own son as a sacrifice but God stepped in and provided the sacrifice in the form of a ram. Abraham built an altar and named it *the Lord will provide*, Jehovah Jireh. Walk in obedience and build an altar in your heart called Jehovah Jireh, *the Lord will provide*. God has not changed one bit since Abraham called him Jehovah Jireh. Not one bit. He is your provider and brings sweetness and satisfaction as you walk in obedience to Him. He has sacrificed His son so Eden is restored in your fellowship with him.

But without faith [it is] impossible to please [him]: for he that cometh to God **must believe that he is**, *and [that]* **he is a rewarder of them that diligently seek him.** -Hebrews 11:6

You seek God by your obedience to His Word. See that faith is believing for if you truly believe, you obey. **The Greek word for faith means** *believing that God is*. If you truly believe and obey, God rewards you with the fullness of His promise, with His faithfulness. The opening words of Hebrews 11:6 are doubly true. Without faith, ours and God's, it is impossible to please Him. We must be faithful to believe that He is, that He simply is. After all, if God is, **and He is**, then the miracle of Him even **being** gives us confidence in every Word he speaks. **If God is**

powerful enough to be, *just to be*, outside of all logic and known science, then He is powerful enough to keep every Word He says. Then, He is faithful to help our faith. The Spirit helps us in our faith, our patience, our abandonment to God and our trust of Him. Now, really, do you think you could have faith if it weren't for the help of the Spirit. Of course not. So, indeed, without faith (faithfulness), His and ours, we cannot please Him. For we do not obey by our own strength, but by yielding to Him who helps our infirmities.

For in this hope we were saved. But hope that is seen is no hope at all. Who hopes for what he already has? But if we hope for what we do not yet have, we wait for it patiently. In the same way, the Spirit helps us in our weakness. We do not know what we ought to pray for, but the Spirit himself intercedes for us with groans that words cannot express. And he who searches our hearts knows the mind of the Spirit, because the Spirit intercedes for the saints in accordance with God's will. And we know that in all things God works for the good of those who love him, who have been called according to his purpose. -Rom 8:24-28 NIV

Do you desire spirit-dominance? Do you yearn to know your place in the Kingdom? Do you want the abundant life promised in Christ? Do you want to be a 30, 60 or even 100- fold producer in the Kingdom, bearing much fruit to the glory of God? Do you want to put the past behind and press toward the mark of your high calling in Christ Jesus? Do you want to find purpose, power and peace? Look to the Spirit of God. He will help you. He will take everything of the past, the present and the future and work it together for good if your heart is pure in your desire.

If you abide in Me, and My words abide in you, you will ask what you desire, and it shall be done for you. By this My Father is glorified, that you bear much fruit; so you will be My disciples. As the Father loved Me, I also have loved you; abide in My love. If you keep My commandments, you will abide in My love, just as I have kept My Father's commandments and abide in His love. These things I have spoken to you, that My joy may remain in you, and that your joy may be full. This is My commandment, that you love one another as I have loved you. —John 15:7-12 NKJV

We're speaking of true abundant life. We're talking about pressing toward the mark of your high calling in Christ. **And we're teaching the path to purpose, power and peace in the Kingdom.**

The thief cometh not, but for to steal, and to kill, and to destroy: I am come that they might have life, and that they might have [it] more abundantly. —John 10:10

Abundant life is not riches or fame. Abundant life is knowing your purpose, the pleasure of God in the Kingdom, living it out in love by His Word, and realizing the peace which accompanies love and purpose in Christ! God will take care of all your needs and if you seek His Kingdom, He will give it to you (Matthew 6:33).

Not as though I had already attained, either were already perfect: but I follow after, if that I may apprehend that for which also I am apprehended of Christ Jesus. Brethren, I count not myself to have apprehended (arrived at perfection): but [this] one thing [I do], forgetting those things which are behind, and reaching forth unto those things which are before, I press toward the mark for the prize of the **high calling of God in Christ Jesus***. —Phil. 3: 12-14*

The **high calling** of every believer must be the same. What!? If our goal is finding our purpose, how can everyone's "high calling" be the same. **Every believer's high calling is God's call to perfected or matured love. To love like God loves. Your high calling and your purpose are two distinct things**. First, you must learn to LOVE God with all your spirit, soul and body. And to love others as God teaches you to love yourself in Him. That is transformation into *Kingdom life* where, as opposed to the strife of earth, there is love for God and love for one another.

That love is your high calling. It is part of the abundance you can know in Christ. But what about your purpose, the specific and unique will of God for your life?

I beseech you therefore, brethren, by the mercies of God, that ye present your bodies a living sacrifice, holy, acceptable unto God, [which is] your reasonable service. **And be not conformed to this world: but be ye transformed by the renewing of your mind, that ye may prove what [is] that good, and acceptable, and perfect, will of God.** *For I say, through the grace given unto me, to every man that is among you, not to think [of himself] more highly than he ought to think; but to think soberly, according as God hath dealt to every man the measure of faith. For as we have many members in one body, and* **all members have not the same office:** *So we, [being] many, are one body in Christ, and every one members one of another. Having then* **gifts differing according to the grace that is given to us**, *whether prophecy, [let us prophesy] according to the proportion of faith; Or ministry, [let us wait] on [our] ministering: or he that teacheth, on teaching; Or he that exhorteth, on exhortation: he that giveth, [let him do it] with simplicity; he that ruleth, with diligence; he that sheweth mercy, with cheerfulness.*
-Romans 12:1-8

Focus on growing in the LOVE of God, in His character. Determine to look into His face, His Word, and reflect His glory, looking progressively like the Father, becoming a partaker of His divine nature (love). As you do, and His love is matured in you, the Holy Spirit will reveal your unique purpose and equip you with every good thing needed to live that purpose out.

Actually, according to scripture, *God will do more than you ask.* Here is our prayer for you, the prayer of Paul for the believer, as you begin or continue a journey toward spirit-dominance, fullness of joy, purpose in the Kingdom, fruition, perfected love, completion, fullness of salvation, sanctification. It is called by many names. **It is found in only one place...the agape' heart of the Father God.**

...I bow my knees unto the Father of our Lord Jesus Christ, Of whom the whole family in heaven and earth is named, That He would grant you, according to the riches of His glory **(God gives like a King, not a pauper)***, to be strengthened with might by His Spirit in the inner man* **(isn't that the clearest reference to spirit dominance we have used?)***; That Christ may dwell* **(when he takes residence, you don't want to sin in his presence)** *in your hearts by faith* **(you must believe in His faithfulness)***; that ye, being rooted and grounded in love,* **(there's the sower and soil again!)** *may be able to comprehend* **(perceive by revelation)** *with all saints what [is] the breadth, and length, and depth, and height;* **(the boundless measures of God's love!)** *And to know the love of Christ, which passeth knowledge* **(it takes a revelation...revelation brings revolution brings transformation)***, that ye might be filled with all the fullness of God.* **(All the fullness of God! That's being a partaker of His divine LOVE nature!)** *Now unto Him that is able to do exceeding abundantly above all that we ask or think,* **(God exceeds our requests and expectations with His abundance)** *according to the power that worketh in us,* **(that's the power of the Word, working by the Holy Spirit in us)***. Unto Him [be] glory in the church by Christ Jesus throughout all ages, world without end. Amen.   –Eph. 3: 15-21*

Jesus Prayed For You!

If you are a believer, a follower of Jesus Christ, Jesus prayed for you before He went to the cross. He met with His disciples to explain what was going to happen. Then, He lifted up His eyes to heaven and began to pray to the Father. A portion of that prayer is printed here from John 17, verses 6-26 (NIV):

I have manifested Your name to the men whom You have given Me out of the world. They were Yours, You gave them to Me, and they have kept Your word. Now they have known that all things which You have given Me are from You. For I have given to them the words which You have given Me; and they have received them, and have known surely that I came forth from

You; and they have believed that You sent Me. I pray for them. I do not pray for the world but for those whom You have given Me, for they are Yours. And all Mine are Yours, and Yours are Mine, and I am glorified in them. Now I am no longer in the world, but these are in the world, and I come to You. **Holy Father, keep through Your name those whom You have given Me, that they may be one as We are.** While I was with them in the world, I kept them in Your name. Those whom You gave Me I have kept; and none of them is lost except the son of perdition, that the Scripture might be fulfilled. But now I come to You, and these things I speak in the world, **that they may have My joy fulfilled in themselves.** I have given them Your word; and the world has hated them because they are not of the world, just as I am not of the world. **I do not pray that You should take them out of the world, but that You should keep them from the evil one.** They are not of the world, just as I am not of the world. **Sanctify them by Your truth. Your word is truth.** As You sent Me into the world, I also have sent them into the world. And for their sakes I sanctify Myself, that they also may be sanctified by the truth. **I do not pray for these alone, but also for those who will believe in Me through their word; that they all may be one, as You, Father, are in Me, and I in You; that they also may be one in Us, that the world may believe that You sent Me.** And the glory which You gave Me I have given them, that they may be one just as We are one: I in them, and You in Me; that they may be made perfect in one, and that the world may know that You have sent Me, and have loved them as You have loved Me. Father, I desire that they also whom You gave Me may be with Me where I am, that they may behold My glory which You have given Me; for You loved Me before the foundation of the world. O righteous Father! The world has not known You, but I have known You; and these have known that You sent Me. And I have declared to them Your name, and will declare it, that the love with which You loved Me may be in them, and I in them.

Note three powerful requests made by Jesus just for you:

First, Jesus prayed that the Father would **KEEP** you by His name. His name means His character. Jesus prayed that the Father would keep you from the enemy by all of His goodness. That's powerful. Second, Jesus prayed that the Father would **SANCTIFY** you, set you apart from the world, by His truth. How powerful is the truth, the Word of God! Paul, in Ephesians 3, called it the "power that worketh in you", the Word working in you to bring about the fullness of salvation in you, to bring you into purpose, power and peace in the Kingdom. Third, Jesus prayed that the Father would bring you into **UNITY** with other believers and with the Godhead. What incredible intimacy! Jesus said the result of this tremendous oneness would be so powerful that the world, those unsaved around you, would believe the Father sent the Son. In other words, they would believe the plan of the Father, the gospel, and become believers.

Let the journey toward spirit-dominance be your greatest joy, knowing that the Father is working the answer to Jesus' prayer in you!

Note one more element of this powerful prayer: *But now I come to You, and these things I speak in the world, that they may have My joy fulfilled in themselves.*

Jesus prayed that you be kept from evil, sanctified for purpose, and brought into unity with the Godhead that you might know the **joy** which Jesus knew. Jesus experienced keeping, sanctification and unity in the Father. Jesus, for all of His sacrifice, knew tremendous joy. Jesus, as He walked the earth, lived the perfect life of purpose, power and peace. Jesus, our example, lived the ultimate spirit dominant life.

He prayed the same for you. He wants you to know the same experience of joy in the Father that He knew. As you continue in your journey, anticipate God's answering Jesus' prayer for you. Let this journey be your greatest joy.

When you walk in your purpose, your place in the Kingdom, God receives glory. When the church comes to fullness, without spot or wrinkle, God will receive ultimate and eternal glory from His church.

A word of warning! When you begin to walk in perfected love, Satan may attempt to pervert your understanding of that love in you and tempt you to become judgmental and spiritually elite or arrogant. This negates the work of perfected love in your spirit. Remember that perfected love will work the fruit of the spirit in you in great measure. Arrogance is not listed in Galatians 5!

But the fruit of the Spirit is ***love, joy, peace, longsuffering, gentleness, goodness, faith, meekness, temperance****: against such there is no law. And they that are Christ's have crucified the flesh with the affections and lusts. If we live in the Spirit, let us also walk in the Spirit. Let us not be desirous of vain glory, provoking one another, envying one another. – Gal 5:22-26*

A person perfected in love will live a bold but humble life. Their demeanor will be one of sweetness and gentleness. Their heart will be one of compassion. If the fruit of the Spirit is not growing in you, perfected love Is not progressing in you. Be very careful, as you grow in the perfection of love, that you not become harsh and impatient with believers who are behind you in their maturing process. Pray for them and speak encouragement to them! Be careful not to condemn them for the very immaturity which you, as a believer, once experienced! The crucifixion of flesh in your life most likely didn't happen overnight; don't demand such instant sanctification in others. If you received a miracle of instant sanctification, something very rare, show your gratitude by patiently assisting others in their journey.

WHERE ARE YOU?

We realize many people will read JOURNEY INTO SPIRIT LIFE but, for this moment, we are concerned for *you*. Where are **YOU** in your journey?

Perhaps you are just beginning your journey as a new believer and want to be all you can be in Christ. You may have struggles to overcome. You may establish goals.

Maybe you are a long-term believer, well into your journey, who desires more fullness of salvation.

Are you a believer who is struggling with unbalanced emotions or physical lust and you desire to know dominance of your spirit?

Does some specific struggle such as illness or disease have you bound?

Is there a sin or are there sins which easily beset you and you have not been able to overcome?

Do relationship conflicts hinder your advancement in your journey?

Are you robbed by an addiction?

Has fear in any form set itself against you? Maybe in the form of doubt, anxiety or depression.

Maybe none of these descriptions fits your place in life. What is your struggle?

What are your spiritual goals?

Search God's Word for the solution to your struggle. Maybe you will find those promises right here in the scriptures we have quoted. Perhaps you will discover them in your Bible. You may be able to find a "promise book" at your Christian bookstore which lists God's promises by category of need. Those little books are great. Once you have found those promises of God, begin to confess them over your need. Write the PROMISE, say the promise of God aloud. Write a confession based on God's promise-Kingdom Truth. For instance, if you have fear, say something like this based on God's Word:

I am a child of the living God. I have not been given the spirit of fear, but of power, love and a sound mind. I will walk in the power of God's Word, the joy of His love and the peace of a sound mind. I have no fear, dread, anxiety or depression. I walk in JOY UNSPEAKABLE AND FULL OF GLORY. The joy of the Lord is my strength.

You will recognize every statement of confession above as scriptural, as KINGDOM TRUTH. Even if your present earthly circumstances do not line up with your statements, believe the confession of KINGDOM TRUTH over earthly circumstance. By your spirit, call your soul and body into agreement with God's promise.

We have offered thirty-one scripture-based confessions in this book. We call this section of the book **THIRTY-ONE DAYS TOWARD GREATER SPIRIT DOMINANCE**. You may want to start with the thirty-one, then write your own. Writing down your own struggle and a scripture-based response of confession will help you overcome!

God has promised us that great things will happen in the lives of JOURNEY readers who embrace His Word. We come into agreement with God's promises for you and with your scripture-based confession of those promises. We trust God to respond to your desire to be spirit dominant, to be more like Him. We would love to hear of your testimony of God's faithfulness in your journey. Please log on to **spiritlifejourney.com**. Click on the **GOD IS FAITHFUL** icon and send us your good report. We look forward to hearing from you and praying for ***you, the chosen of God!***

Thirty One Days Toward Greater Spirit Dominance

Scripture-based confessions to bring you into greater harmony of spirit, soul & body.

Confession – Day One

For God so loved the world, that he gave his only begotten Son, that whosoever believeth in him should not perish, but have everlasting life. –John 3:16

Jesus saith unto him, I am the way, the truth, and the life: no man cometh unto the Father, but by me.   -John 14:6

I believe on Jesus, the Son of God, for my salvation. I believe in God, the Creator of everything. I believe God sent His Son, Jesus, part of the TRINITY, out from Himself. God's WORD became flesh in Jesus, and Jesus dwelled among men, doing good works, reflecting the character of the Father upon the earth. It was the plan of the Father that Jesus suffer and die on the cross, conforming not to His will but to the will of His Father, that all men might have the opportunity to be reconciled to fellowship with God through Christ. There is no other plan of salvation and reconciliation to God outside Jesus. I believe Jesus was resurrected and lives at the right hand of the Father, making intercession for me that I might have life and have it abundantly, in fullness, upon the earth. I also believe I will have everlasting life when my spirit transitions from earth into the presence of God in heaven upon the death of my body or the return of Jesus for His church.

Confession – Day Two

For by grace are ye saved through faith; and that not of yourselves: [it is] the gift of God: Not of works, lest any man should boast. –Eph. 2: 8-9

Therefore if any man [be] in Christ, [he is] a new creature: old things are passed away; behold, all things are become new. -- 2 Cor. 5:17

Are ye so foolish? having begun in the Spirit, are ye now made perfect by the flesh? --Gal 3:3

For in this hope we were saved. But hope that is seen is no hope at all. Who hopes for what he already has? But if we hope for what we do not yet have, we wait for it patiently. In the same way, the Spirit helps us in our weakness. We do not know what we ought to pray for, but the Spirit himself intercedes for us with groans that words cannot express. And he who searches our hearts knows the mind of the Spirit, because the Spirit intercedes for the saints in accordance with God's will. And we know that in all things God works for the good of those who love him, who have been called according to his purpose. --Rom 8:24-28 NIV

I am a new person. My old nature is progressively passing away and my new nature in Christ is emerging. I could not save myself; I can not keep myself and I can not grow myself in God. I am incapable of works great enough to reconcile myself to the Almighty God for God alone is good. Whatever good I exhibit in life is a gift from Him. It is God's grace which saved me upon my believing in His faithfulness. I will never boast in self but will always boast in God to give Him glory and honor. My keeping and maturing as a believer comes from God just as my salvation came from God. God sends the Holy Spirit to work maturity in me, step-by-step or from level to level, glory to glory. I believe the Holy Spirit will work in me to grow me into everything God desires me to be. Because God loves me and I love Him, and He has purpose for my life, He works all things in my life together for good.

Confession – Day Three

How excellent [is] thy lovingkindness, O God! therefore the children of men put their trust under the shadow of thy wings. -Ps. 36:7

But without faith [it is] impossible to please [him]: for he that cometh to God must believe that he is, and [that] he is a rewarder of them that diligently seek him. --Hebrews 11:6

Bless the LORD, O my soul; and all that is within me, bless His holy name! Bless the LORD, O my soul, and forget not all His benefits: who forgives all your iniquities, who heals all your diseases, who redeems your life from destruction, who crowns you with lovingkindness and tender mercies, who satisfies your mouth with good things, so that your youth is renewed like the eagle's. The LORD executes righteousness and justice for all who are oppressed. He made known His ways to Moses, His acts to the children of Israel. The LORD is merciful and gracious, slow to anger, and abounding in mercy. He will not always strive with us, nor will He keep His anger forever. He has not dealt with us according to our sins,nor punished us according to our iniquities. For as the heavens are high above the earth, so great is His mercy toward those who fear Him; as far as the east is from the west, so far has He removed our transgressions from us. As a father pities his children,so the LORD pities those who fear Him. For He knows our frame; He remembers that we are dust. As for man, his days are like grass; as a flower of the field, so he flourishes. For the wind passes over it, and it is gone, and its place remembers it no moreBut the mercy of the LORD is from everlasting to everlasting on those who fear Him, and His righteousness to children's children, to such as keep His covenant, and to those who remember His commandments to do them. - Psa 103:2-18 NKJV

I trust God completely in every area of my life. God watches over me and overshadows me so I am safe. Because I believe in Him with my whole heart, He rewards me with His favor. I please Him. The benefits of my salvation are many and I count them often so that I am not tempted to take them lightly and I do not fail to pursue them diligently in the Spirit. God is the father of every good gift and has plans to prosper me and never to harm me. God desires good things for me and delights (pleasures) in my fullness. I bring the desires of my heart into agreement with those of the Father who has my very best interest in mind.

Confession – Day Four

Neither shall they say, Lo here or, lo there for, behold, the kingdom of God is within you. -Luke 17:21

As for you, the anointing you received from him remains in you, and you do not need anyone to teach you. But as his anointing teaches you about all things and as that anointing is real, not counterfeit—just as it has taught you, remain in him.
–I John 2:27 NIV

But if the Spirit of Him who raised Jesus from the dead dwells in you, He who raised Christ from the dead will also give life to your mortal bodies through His Spirit who dwells in you.
-Romans 8:11 NKJV

Likewise reckon ye also yourselves to be dead indeed unto sin, but alive unto God through Jesus Christ our Lord.
–Romans 6:11

I will not make the mistake of looking for the Kingdom of God to be manifested physically as if God is going to lower a physical kingdom upon the earth. Rather, as a believer, I believe the Kingdom of God has been planted in me as a seed, His Word, and grows in me by the working of the Spirit in my human spirit. While I appreciate the teaching of anointed men and women, I acknowledge the Holy Spirit as my Teacher and look to Him to grow the Kingdom in me to make my purpose in the Kingdom full and complete. The Holy Spirit abides in me and teaches me truth, growing me from level to level of glory. My body, my flesh, is quickened by the same resurrection power that raised Jesus from the dead. I am quickened unto life in God through Christ.

This life is defined in scripture as true, active, blessed, endless, vital, fresh, vigorous, powerful and efficient. As I cooperate, allowing the Spirit to work the Word of God in me, I will progressively and aggressively become more alive and more aware of my purpose in the Kingdom of God.

Confession – Day Five

What shall we say, then? Shall we go on sinning so that grace may increase? By no means! We died to sin; how can we live in it any longer? Or don't you know that all of us who were baptized into Christ Jesus were baptized into his death? We were therefore buried with him through baptism into death in order that, just as Christ was raised from the dead through the glory of the Father, we too may live a new life. If we have been united with him like this in his death, we will certainly also be united with him in his resurrection. For we know that our old self was crucified with him so that the body of sin might be done away with,[a] that we should no longer be slaves to sin—because anyone who has died has been freed from sin. Now if we died with Christ, we believe that we will also live with him. For we know that since Christ was raised from the dead, he cannot die again; death no longer has mastery over him. The death he died, he died to sin once for all; but the life he lives, he lives to God. In the same way, count yourselves dead to sin but alive to God in Christ Jesus. Therefore do not let sin reign in your mortal body so that you obey its evil desires. Do not offer the parts of your body to sin, as instruments of wickedness, but rather offer yourselves to God, as those who have been brought from death to life; and offer the parts of your body to him as instruments of righteousness. For sin shall not be your master, because you are not under law, but under grace. –Romans 6: 1-14 NIV

The sinful mind is hostile to God. It does not submit to God's law, nor can it do so. Those controlled by the sinful nature cannot please God. You, however, are controlled not by the sinful nature but by the Spirit, if the Spirit of God lives in you. And if anyone does not have the Spirit of Christ, he does not belong to Christ.

But if Christ is in you, your body is dead because of sin, yet your spirit is alive because of righteousness. And if the Spirit of him who raised Jesus from the dead is living in you, he who raised Christ from the dead will also give life to your mortal bodies through his Spirit, who lives in you. Therefore, brothers, we have an obligation—but it is not to the sinful nature, to live according to it. For if you live according to the sinful nature, you will die; but if by the Spirit you put to death the misdeeds of the body, you will live, because those who are led by the Spirit of God are sons of God. -- Romans 8: 7-14 NIV

It is not God's will that I live in sin. One of the benefits of my salvation is freedom from sin. It has no dominion over me as I believe and obey the Word of God. I am tempted to sin only when I give place to flesh over spirit. I reckon myself to be alive, full of the life of God, through Christ, and reject the resurrection of flesh in me. I crucify flesh and yield every part of my spirit, soul and body unto God as instruments of righteousness. As I do so, I exhibit His character and walk in His pleasure. If I sin, I do not take it lightly and I come quickly to repentance, calling upon God for forgiveness. Forgiven and refusing to walk in condemnation, I return quickly to my place in the Spirit and continue my forward walk in Christ.

Confession – Day Six

Not that I have already attained, or am already perfected; but I press on, that I may lay hold of that for which Christ Jesus has also laid hold of me. Brethren, I do not count myself to have apprehended; but one thing I do, forgetting those things which are behind and reaching forward to those things which are ahead, I press toward the goal for the prize of the upward call of God in Christ Jesus. -- Phil. 3: 12-14 NKJV

While I learn from the past, I will not live in the past. Certainly, I will not live in the guilt of past sin. Having repented and received the grace of God, I press forward toward the mark of the prize of the high calling of God in Christ Jesus. My high calling is the agape' love of God. I will strive for perfection in that love by allowing the Holy Spirit to lead me into all truth.

Confession – Day Seven

Therefore, I urge you, brothers, in view of God's mercy, to offer your bodies as living sacrifices, holy and pleasing to God—this is your spiritual act of worship. Do not conform any longer to the pattern of this world, but be transformed by the renewing of your mind. Then you will be able to test and approve what God's will is—his good, pleasing and perfect will. For by the grace given me I say to every one of you: Do not think of yourself more highly than you ought, but rather think of yourself with sober judgment, in accordance with the measure of faith God has given you. Just as each of us has one body with many members, and these members do not all have the same function, so in Christ we who are many form one body, and each member belongs to all the others. We have different gifts, according to the grace given us. If a man's gift is prophesying, let him use it in proportion to his[b]faith. If it is serving, let him serve; if it is teaching, let him teach; if it is encouraging, let him encourage; if it is contributing to the needs of others, let him give generously; if it is leadership, let him govern diligently; if it is showing mercy, let him do it cheerfully.   –Romans 12:1-8 NIV

For they that are after the flesh (body + soul) do mind the things of the flesh; but they that are after the Spirit the things of the Spirit. For to be carnally (concentrating on the flesh) minded [is] death; but to be spiritually minded [is] life and peace. –Romans 8: 5-6

I give myself to God as a living sacrifice, refusing to be conformed to the ways of the earth, I embrace the transforming work of the Holy Spirit in my life. My mind is renewed, passing from thoughts of sin and death to thoughts of righteousness and life. I open myself to the power of God's Word in me as the Holy Spirit transforms me into the pleasure of God. His good and acceptable plan for my life is unfolded day by day as I believe in and love God with my whole heart. I will walk in the fullness of God's plan and gift for my life, serving Him well and bringing Him pleasure.

Confession – Day Eight

But seek ye first the kingdom of God, and his righteousness; and all these things shall be added unto you. - Romans 6:33

My desire is to know fullness of the Kingdom of God in my life, to know His character matured in me that I might reflect His glory to others. While God cares for my material needs, my focus is on seeking His Kingdom and His righteousness. God will give me those things I focus on. As I give the pursuit of His Kingdom and righteousness my attention, God will give those to me. God is the giver of every good gift and will give me righteousness as I hunger for it. My life will be full, satisfying and fruitful to His glory.

Confession – Day Nine

While a large crowd was gathering and people were coming to Jesus from town after town, he told this parable: "A farmer went out to sow his seed. As he was scattering the seed, some fell along the path; it was trampled on, and the birds of the air ate it up. Some fell on rock, and when it came up, the plants withered because they had no moisture. Other seed fell among thorns, which grew up with it and choked the plants. Still other seed fell on good soil. It came up and yielded a crop, a hundred times more than was sown." When he said this, he called out, "He who has ears to hear, let him hear." His disciples asked him what this parable meant. He said, "The knowledge of the secrets of the kingdom of God has been given to you, but to others I speak in parables, so that, " 'though seeing, they may not see; though hearing, they may not understand.'"This is the meaning of the parable: The seed is the word of God. Those along the path are the ones who hear, and then the devil comes and takes away the word from their hearts, so that they may not believe and be saved. Those on the rock are the ones who receive the word with joy when they hear it, but they have no root. They believe for a while, but in the time of testing they fall away. The seed that fell among thorns stands for those who hear, but as they go on their way they are choked by life's worries, riches and pleasures, and they do not mature. But the seed on good soil stands for those with a noble and good heart, who hear the word, retain it, and by persevering produce a crop. –Luke 8: 4-15 NIV

But he that received seed into the good ground is he that heareth the word, and understandeth [it]; which also beareth fruit, and bringeth forth, some an hundredfold, some sixty, some thirty. --Mat 13:23

God reveals the mysteries of the Kingdom to me. His Kingdom has been invested in me, planted in me, as a seed is planted in good soil. I am good soil, welcoming His Kingdom, protecting and nurturing the seed. My heart is a multiplier, bringing multiplied glory to God. I have an honest and good heart, God's heart, desiring the heart of God to be magnified in me. I receive the Word of God into my whole being and believe it, keeping it in obedience. As I do, it brings forth fruit or completion in my life. My life becomes enriched with purpose as I wait patiently for God to grow Kingdom purpose inside me. As I patiently and diligently walk in obedience, His Word is multiplied and my life brings fruit multiplied thirty, sixty and one-hundred times over His original investment in me. Purpose, power and peace are mine just as He promises.

Confession – Day Ten

And one of the scribes came, and having heard them reasoning together, and perceiving that he had answered them well, asked him, Which is the first commandment of all? And Jesus answered him, The first of all the commandments [is], Hear, O Israel; The Lord our God is one Lord: And thou shalt love the Lord thy God with all thy * <u>heart</u>, and with all thy <u>soul</u>, and with all thy <u>mind</u>, and with all thy <u>strength</u> [spirit, soul and body]: this [is] the first commandment. –Mark 12: 28-30

For the word of God [is] quick, and powerful, and sharper than any twoedged sword, piercing even to the dividing asunder of soul and spirit, and of the joints and marrow, and [is] a discerner of the thoughts and intents of the heart.   —Hebrews 4:12

As God is made up of three parts, so am I. If I am to love God with all my spirit, soul and body, I must be aware of the role of each in my being. I look to the Word of God to reveal the division of each and their purpose in my being. I confess my spirit as dominant with my soul and body following in harmony. I refuse to be dominated by my emotions or weak human reasoning. I will have the mind of Christ. I will grow in my love for God in my tri-part being and will be taught by the Holy Spirit to honor God in my spirit. God is spirit and I must worship Him in spirit if I am to communicate most effectually to Him. My spirit will communicate with God and my reasonings, emotions and physical desires will not hinder our communication. Rather, my whole being will passionately desire God and aggressively and progressively express my love for Him.

Confession – Day Eleven

For ye have not received the spirit of bondage again to fear; but ye have received the Spirit of adoption, whereby we cry, Abba, Father. The Spirit itself beareth witness with our spirit, that we are the children of God. —Romans 8: 15-16

There is no fear in love; but perfect love casteth out fear: because fear hath torment. He that feareth is not made perfect in love. - I John 4:18

For God hath not given us the spirit of fear; but of power, and of love, and of a sound mind. - II Tim 1:17

The LORD [is] my light and my salvation; whom shall I fear? the LORD [is] the strength of my life; of whom shall I be afraid? - Psalm 27:1

I am a child of God. The Spirit bears witness with my spirit that I am adopted into the Kingdom of God and call God, Father. He is the light and strength of my life. I have absolutely nothing and no one to fear. I need not live in anxiety or dread. I reject discouragement and depression which are forms of fear. Since my life is increasingly filled with the love of God and I am being perfected in that love, there is no place for fear. I live in power, love and a sound mind-power that is inherent in my Father's character. Love that is my Father's character. I have a sound mind that encourages a life of self-control and positive thoughts. Since I am released from fear, I am released unto a more fruitful and pleasant life. Walking free from fear, I am free to express the love of God more freely to those around me.

Confession – Day Twelve

Casting down imaginations, and every high thing that exalteth itself against the knowledge of God, and bringing into captivity every thought to the obedience of Christ. - II Cor. 10:5

For who hath known the mind of the Lord, that he may instruct him? But we have the mind of Christ.   – I Cor 2:16

Finally, brethren, whatsoever things are true, whatsoever things [are] honest, whatsoever things [are] just, whatsoever things [are] pure, whatsoever things [are] lovely, whatsoever things [are] of good report; if [there be] any virtue, and if [there be] any praise, think on these things. – Phil 4:8

When imaginations come that challenge the Truth of God, I will reject them. I will not allow them to take up residence in my soul (mind) but will instead dwell on the teachings of Christ which counter such lies. Before my new birth in Christ, my mind tended to dwell on negative things. I will now think on positive things, things which are based on the Word of God which is Truth. I will now think on things which are honest, reflecting the integrity of God. I will think on things which are just according to the laws of God. I will think on things which are pure, not soiled with the selfish thoughts of earth. I will think on things which are lovely, bringing peace and pleasure to my mind. I will think on things which are of good report, filled with faith and assurance. I will think on things which are virtuous, morally excellent and free from lustful thoughts. I will be careful to praise those who deserve it and never tear down my fellow man. Above all, I will praise God who is always worthy of praise. My mind is set free by my obedience to Christ and I will think as He does from a heart of love.

Confession – Day Thirteen

Be joyful always; pray continually; give thanks in all circumstances, for this is God's will for you in Christ Jesus. Do not put out the Spirit's fire; do not treat prophecies with contempt. Test everything. Hold on to the good. Avoid every kind of evil. May God himself, the God of peace, sanctify you through and through. May your whole spirit, soul and body be kept blameless at the coming of our Lord Jesus Christ. The one who calls you is faithful and he will do it. - I Th 5: 16-24 NIV

And we know that all things work together for good to them that love God, to them who are the called according to [his] purpose. –Romans 8:28

My life is one of constant rejoicing and prayer. I live in a spirit of joy and prayer. In every situation of life, I give thanks, for to live in an attitude of thanksgiving is God's desire for my life. God will take every situation of my life, even my failures, and work them all together for good in my life as I fully trust Him. God has called me to be His child and will mature and perfect me to His pleasure. I embrace the things of God fully and trust Him to do in me everything His Word promises. As I do so, the Father progressively matures my spirit, bringing me into the more perfect harmony of my spirit, soul and body. This results in synergy, the harmonious flow of life in my tri-part being, which produces a more fruitful and peaceful life. My life will be increasingly full, free and productive right up to the coming of my Lord Jesus or my passing from this life unto His perfect presence.

Confession – Day Fourteen

And be not conformed to this world: but be ye transformed by the renewing of your mind [this is a work of the Holy Spirit], that ye may prove what [is] that good, and acceptable, and perfect will of God [in your life]. -Romans 12:2

But we all, with open face beholding as in a glass the glory of the Lord, are changed into the same image from glory to glory, [even] as by the Spirit of the Lord. - 2 Cor. 3:18

For the word of God [is] quick, and powerful, and sharper than any twoedged sword, piercing even to the dividing asunder of soul and spirit, and of the joints and marrow, and [is] a discerner of the thoughts and intents of the heart. – Hebrew 4:12

Now unto him that is able to do exceeding abundantly above all that we ask or think, according to the power that worketh in us, Unto him [be] glory in the church by Christ Jesus throughout all ages, world without end. Amen. – Hebrews 3:20-21

The thief cometh not, but for to steal, and to kill, and to destroy: I am come that they might have life, and that they might have [it] more abundantly. – John 10:10

I will not be conformed to this world which is death but will be transformed by the Word of God which is life. It is God's plan that I have a more abundant life through Jesus. Transformation is not something I can do but rather is something I must attain through cooperation with the Holy Spirit. The Holy Spirit applies God's Word to me. This application of the Word, the power that works in me, reveals the proper roles of spirit, soul and body in my life. This brings the purpose and pleasure, the perfect will of God, for my life. This process of transformation is not something I must strive for, but something I must cooperate with. It is the Holy Spirit's responsibility to transform me by the renewing of my mind to Kingdom Truth as I consume the Word of God.

Confession – Day Fifteen

For my yoke [is] easy, and my burden is light   -Matthew 11:30.

If the Son therefore shall make you free, ye shall be free indeed. –John 8:36

For the law of the Spirit of life in Christ Jesus hath made me free from the law of sin and death.   –Romans 8:2

Blessed [are] they which do hunger and thirst after ighteousness: for they shall be filled. -Matthew 5:6

This thing of following Jesus is not burdensome. Rather, it brings life and liberty. While the world believes the lie that being anchored in the teachings of Jesus brings bondage, I know I have been set free from the law of sin and death. Sin no longer rules in me. Therefore, death no longer rules in me. Instead of progressively dying, I am progressively living! I live in greater power and peace, not bound to the death this world affords, but bound to, yoked to, the giver of life! The burden of earthly life has lifted as I am set free by the giver of abundant and eternal life!

Confession – Day Sixteen

*And one of the scribes came, and having heard them reasoning together, and perceiving that he had answered them well, asked him, Which is the first commandment of all? And Jesus answered him, The first of all the commandments [is], Hear, O Israel; The Lord our God is one Lord: And thou shalt love the Lord thy God with all thy * <u>heart</u>, and with all thy <u>soul</u>, and with all thy <u>mind,</u> and with all thy <u>strength</u> [spirit, soul and body]: this [is] the first commandment.   –Matthew 12:28-30*

For this is the love of God, that we keep his commandments: and his commandments are not grievous.   –I John 5:3

Then said they unto him, What shall we do, that we might work

the works of God? Jesus answered and said unto them, This is the work of God, that ye believe on him whom he hath sent.
—John 6: 28-29

Let this mind be in you, which was also in Christ Jesus.
—Phil. 2:5

I believe God with my whole heart. God was and is and forever will be. I have eternal life in Him. I will live in His presence forever. I obey because He loves me and wants the very best for me. I learn to do the works of God, living out His character toward others, by loving Him in my whole being. In my spirit which communicates with Him, spirit to spirit, for God is spirit. In my emotions and reasonings which would love to run amok but are tamed by the Holy Spirit, working the mind of Christ in me. In my body, which is brought into discipline and submission that I might live a wholesome and healthy life before God. Every area of my life expresses love for God and for my fellow man. This is not hard but brings joy and peace!

Confession – Day Seventeen

But my servant Caleb, because he had another spirit with him, and hath followed me fully, him will I bring into the land whereinto he went; and his seed shall possess it. -Num. 14:24

Save Caleb the son of Jephunneh the Kenezite, and Joshua the son of Nun: for they have wholly followed the LORD. -Num. 13:12

But let him ask in faith, nothing wavering. For he that wavereth is like a wave of the sea driven with the wind and tossed. For let not that man think that he shall receive any thing of the Lord. A double minded man [is] unstable in all his ways. —James 1:6-8

I have a Caleb spirit. I believe God's promise with all my spirit, soul and body. If God promised it, God will perform it. I am not persuaded by the struggles and obstacles of earth but trust God to overcome. I will follow God fully, without reservation. I will be single-minded that I might receive from God and do the good works of God. By following God fully, having *another* spirit, I will live out God's full pleasure. My life will be full, satisfying, fruitful and God-glorifying. I will not stop short of God's Promised Land for my life but will know it and possess it completely. I will not be denied but I will possess the land promised me and know the fullness, the land of milk and honey, in my life. Through faith, patience, abandonment and trust in God, I overcome the corruption of earth.

Confession – Day Eighteen

If ye love me, keep my commandments. –John 14:5

If ye keep my commandments, ye shall abide in my love; even as I have kept my Father's commandments, and abide in his love. Verily, verily, I say unto you, He that believeth on me, the works that I do shall he do also; and greater [works] than these shall he do; because I go unto my Father. –John 15:10-12

Jesus obeyed God. He kept the Father's commandments. I see the power which obedience worked in HIS life! Jesus said I would do the works He did and greater! How can this be! The fullness of God's plan in my life, my life being ruled by spirit and doing the great works of love, are accomplished through obedience. God sees my obedience as proof of my faith in Him and love for Him. There is unity, an abiding, which comes from my obedience. Because I believe with all my heart, manifesting that belief in obedience to His Word, God abides in me and I in Him. There is unity of purpose. His character becomes mine and I live out His love for others! This brings great satisfaction, real joy, to my life.

Confession – Day Nineteen

For the kingdom of God is not a matter of eating and drinking, but of righteousness, peace and joy in the Holy Spirit. –Romans 14:17 NIV

And the peace of God, which passeth all understanding, shall keep your hearts and minds through Christ Jesus. —Phillipians 4:7

And these things write we unto you, that your joy may be full. —I John 1:4

And be found in him, not having mine own righteousness, which is of the law, but that which is through the faith of Christ, the righteousness which is of God by faith: -Phil. 3:9

Neither shall they say, Lo here! or, lo there! for, behold, the kingdom of God is within you. —Luke 17:21

The Kingdom of God is within me, placed there by the Holy Spirit in response to my believing on Jesus. I will not look to meat or drink-legalism, man-made rules-as evidence of the Kingdom of God in my life. The Kingdom of God within me will be expressed and manifested by God's righteousness, God's supernatural peace and fullness of joy. The Kingdom will grow in me, not by my human effort but by my cooperation with the Holy Spirit.

Confession – Day Twenty

Therefore, since we are surrounded by such a great cloud of witnesses, let us throw off everything that hinders and the sin that so easily entangles, and let us run with perseverance the race marked out for us. Let us fix our eyes on Jesus, the author and perfecter of our faith, who for the joy set before him endured the cross, scorning its shame, and sat down at the right hand of the throne of God. —Hebrews 12:1-2 NIV

Now faith is the substance of things hoped for, the evidence of things not seen. —Hebrews 11:1

Even so faith, if it hath not works, is dead, being alone. Yea, a man may say, Thou hast faith, and I have works: shew me thy faith without thy works, and I will shew thee my faith by my works. —James 2:17-18

For by grace are ye saved through faith; and that not of yourselves: [it is] the gift of God: Not of works, lest any man should boast. –Eph. 2:8-9

Therefore [we are] always confident, knowing that, whilst we are at home in the body, we are absent from the Lord: (For we walk by faith, not by sight:)   -II Cor. 5:6-7

And Jesus said unto them, Because of your unbelief: for verily I say unto you, If ye have faith as a grain of mustard seed, ye shall say unto this mountain, Remove hence to yonder place; and it shall remove; and nothing shall be impossible unto you. –Matthew 17:20

Like the disciples, I have no faith of my own. Whatever faith I have is a gift from God. Only God is absolutely faithful so only God, the giver of all good gifts, can give faith. He breathes faith into me. My faith is expressed by believing that God is and will do all He has promised. Because I believe in His faithfulness, I respond in obedience with works of His expressed love. When earthly fact clashes with Kingdom truth, I will, by faith, choose Kingdom truth, walking by faith and not by sight. I will call things that are not as though they are, always believing God above the ways and thoughts of man.

Confession – Day Twenty-One

Whoever confesses that Jesus is the Son of God, God abides in him, and he in God. And we have known and believed the love that God has for us. God is love, and he who abides in love abides in God, and God in him. Love has been perfected among us in this: that we may have boldness in the day of judgment; because as He is, so are we in this world. There is no fear in love; but perfect love casts out fear, because fear involves torment. But he who fears has not been made perfect in love. We love Him because He first loved us. If someone says, "I love God," and hates his brother, he is a liar; for he who does not love his brother whom he has seen, how can he love God whom he has not seen? And this commandment we have from Him: that he who loves God must love his brother also. —I John 4:15-21 NKJV

For God hath not given us the spirit of fear; but of power, and of love, and of a sound mind. -2Ti 1:7

You belong to your father, the devil, and you want to carry out your father's desire. He was a murderer from the beginning, not holding to the truth, for there is no truth in him. When he lies, he speaks his native language, for he is a liar and the father of lies. - John 8:44 NIV

Satan is my enemy. He is a liar who desires to rob me by fear and insecurity. Satan cannot defeat me. Only fear and doubt multiplied can defeat me. As I grow in God, in His love, fear and insecurity melt away. I walk in greater love and power and I have the mind of Christ. I refuse the spirit of fear and I am filled with the love of God for others. I will walk in the high calling of love and will increasingly become a partaker of the divine Nature of God. God will open doors and I will boldly walk through them, progressively entering into God's purpose for my life.

Confession – Day Twenty-Two

For the earnest expectation of the creature waiteth for the manifestation of the sons of God. —Roman 8:19

Being confident of this very thing, that he which hath begun a good work in you will perform [it] until the day of Jesus Christ: -Phil. 1:6

And the very God of peace sanctify you wholly; and [I pray God] your whole spirit and soul and body be preserved blameless unto the coming of our Lord Jesus Christ. Faithful [is] he that calleth you, who also will do [it]. —I Thes. 5:23-24

For we are his workmanship, created in Christ Jesus unto good works, which God hath before ordained that we should walk in them. –Eph. 2:10

It gives me great freedom knowing that I am not ultimately responsible for my completion. God who began this good work of salvation, His pleasure in me, is faithful to finish that work. My responsibility is simply to stay in agreement with the Word of God which the Spirit works in me to manifest God's work of sanctification or completion in me. My responsibility is obedience. I will cooperate with the Spirit of God, being confident that He is faithful to sanctify (complete) me wholly in my calling and purpose.

Confession – Day Twenty-Three

But I, by your great mercy, will come into your house; in reverence will I bow down toward your holy temple. –Psalm 5:7 NIV

Give unto the LORD the glory due unto his name; worship the LORD in the beauty of holiness. -Psa 29:2

So shall the king greatly desire thy beauty: for he [is] thy Lord; and worship thou him. -Ps. 45:11

But the hour cometh, and now is, when the true worshippers shall worship the Father in spirit and in truth: for the Father seeketh such to worship him. God [is] a Spirit: and they that worship him must worship [him] in spirit and in truth. –John 4:23-24

I am created to be a worshipper of the living God. My worship, when mature, will be expressed from my human spirit to God who is spirit. My mind and body will follow in harmony with my spirit as I worship in spirit and in truth as a true worshipper. As the Holy Spirit helps me, I will worship more creatively and fervently as I grow from level to level in my walk with God. I refuse to be inhibited in worship and call my flesh into full cooperation with my spirit in worship.

Confession – Day Twenty-Four

But if ye be led of the Spirit, ye are not under the law. Now the works of the flesh are manifest, which are [these]; Adultery, fornication, uncleanness, lasciviousness, idolatry, witchcraft, hatred, variance, emulations, wrath, strife, seditions, heresies, envyings, murders, drunkenness, revellings, and such like: of the which I tell you before, as I have also told [you] in time past, that they which do such things shall not inherit the kingdom of God. But the fruit of the Spirit is love, joy, peace, longsuffering, gentleness, goodness, faith, meekness, temperance: against such there is no law. And they that are Christ's have crucified the flesh with the affections and lusts. If we live in the Spirit, let us also walk in the Spirit. Let us not be desirous of vain glory, provoking one another, envying one another. –Gal. 5:18-26

Whereby are given unto us exceeding great and precious promises: that by these ye might be partakers of the divine nature, having escaped the corruption that is in the world through lust. And beside this, giving all diligence, add to your faith virtue; and to virtue knowledge; And to knowledge temperance; and to temperance patience; and to patience godliness; And to godliness brotherly kindness; and to brotherly kindness charity. For if these things be in you, and abound, they make [you that ye shall] neither [be] barren nor unfruitful in the knowledge of our Lord Jesus Christ. -2 Peter 1:4-8

The fruit of the Spirit are words which describe God's character. God's character grows in me by the Spirit's application of the power that works in me (God's Word) and my cooperation to receive it. In Christ, I escape the corruption of this earth which would seek to bring dominance to my flesh and rob me of purity and purpose in my life. My life as a believer will reflect God's character as the Holy Spirit truly recreates me in God's image. As I embrace the Word of God, I will grow in the character of

God that others might see Jesus in me. As Jesus reflected the glory of the Father on earth, so will I.

Confession – Day Twenty-Five

*Love never fails. But where there are prophecies, they will cease; where there are tongues, they will be stilled; where there is knowledge, it will pass away. For we know in part and we prophesy in part, but when perfection comes, the imperfect disappears. When I was a child, I talked like a child, I thought like a child, I reasoned like a child. When I became a man, I put childish ways behind me. Now we see but a poor reflection as in a mirror; then we shall see face to face. Now I know in part; then I shall know fully, even as I am fully known. And now these three remain: faith, hope and love. But the greatest of these is love.
–I Cor. 13: 8-13 NIV*

*I pray that out of his glorious riches he may strengthen you with power through his Spirit in your inner being, so that Christ may dwell in your hearts through faith. And I pray that you, being rooted and established in love, may have power, together with all the saints, to grasp how wide and long and high and deep is the love of Christ, and to know this love that surpasses knowledge— that you may be filled to the measure of all the fullness of God.
–Ephesians 3: 16-19 NIV*

*But if anyone obeys his word, God's love[a] is truly made complete in him. This is how we know we are in him:
–I John 2:5 NIV*

Beloved, let us love one another: for love is of God; and every one that loveth is born of God, and knoweth God. He that loveth not knoweth not God; for God is love. –I John 4:7-8

If they obey and serve [him], they shall spend their days in prosperity, and their years in pleasures. –Job 36:11

Thou wilt shew me the path of life: in thy presence [is] fulness of joy; at thy right hand [there are] pleasures for evermore.
–Psalm 16:11

God is love and His character flows from His heart of love. The more I grow in relationship with Him, the Word becoming more engrafted in me, I am matured in His love. Any spiritual gift I may be blessed with must be rooted and grounded in His love to be most effectual. As Gods' Word grows in me, my capacity to express His love will be magnified until I become an extension of God's heart flowing to others. My ultimate goal is God's love. Walking in obedience, I will learn the pleasures of God, enjoying a fullness of joy which only those in harmony with the Father can know.

Confession – Day Twenty-Six

But every man is tempted, when he is drawn away of his own lust, and enticed. Then when lust hath conceived, it bringeth forth sin: and sin, when it is finished, bringeth forth death.
–James 1:14-15

Therefore, there is now no condemnation for those who are in Christ Jesus, because through Christ Jesus the law of the Spirit of life set me free from the law of sin and death. For what the law was powerless to do in that it was weakened by the sinful nature, God did by sending his own Son in the likeness of sinful man to be a sin offering. And so he condemned sin in sinful man, in order that the righteous requirements of the law might be fully met in us, who do not live according to the sinful nature but according to the Spirit. Those who live according to the sinful nature have their minds set on what that nature desires; but those who live in accordance with the Spirit have their minds set on what the Spirit desires. The mind of sinful man[e] is death, but the mind controlled by the Spirit is life and peace; *–Rom. 8:1-6*

I have moments of weakness in my flesh when I am tempted to disobey the Word of God. It is the law of sin and death trying to reclaim place in me. If I sin, I will be quick in the assurance of God's forgiveness. I will not wallow in guilt and condemnation. There is no condemnation for I am in Christ. Just as Paul faced a battle between flesh and spirit, so do I. I will repent immediately of sin in my life and will be renewed to walk after the Spirit and not after my flesh. I choose to be spiritually minded, progressively and aggressively rejecting the law of sin and death, and walking in life and peace in Christ.

Confession – Day Twenty-Seven

And to know the love of Christ, which passeth knowledge, that ye might be filled with all the fulness of God. Now unto him that is able to do exceeding abundantly above all that we ask or think, according to the power that worketh in us, Unto him [be] glory in the church by Christ Jesus throughout all ages, world without end. Amen. –Eph. 3:19-21

So I tell you this, and insist on it in the Lord, that you must no longer live as the Gentiles do, in the futility of their thinking. They are darkened in their understanding and separated from the life of God because of the ignorance that is in them due to the hardening of their hearts. Having lost all sensitivity, they have given themselves over to sensuality so as to indulge in every kind of impurity, with a continual lust for more. You, however, did not come to know Christ that way. Surely you heard of him and were taught in him in accordance with the truth that is in Jesus. You were taught, with regard to your former way of life, to put off your old self, which is being corrupted by its deceitful desires; to be made new in the attitude of your minds; and to put on the new self, created to be like God in true righteousness and holiness. --Eph. 4:17-24 NIV

For the wrath of man worketh not the righteousness of God. Wherefore lay apart all filthiness and superfluity of naughtiness, and receive with meekness the engrafted word, which is able to save your souls. But be ye doers of the word, and not hearers only, deceiving your own selves. For if any be a hearer of the word, and not a doer, he is like unto a man beholding his natural face in a glass: For he beholdeth himself, and goeth his way, and straightway forgetteth what manner of man he was. But whoso looketh into the perfect law of liberty, and continueth [therein], he being not a forgetful hearer, but a doer of the work, this man shall be blessed in his deed. —James 1:20-25

Now the Lord is that Spirit: and where the Spirit of the Lord [is], there [is] liberty. But we all, with open face beholding as in a glass the glory of the Lord, are changed into the same image from glory to glory, [even] as by the Spirit of the Lord. —II Cor. 3:17-18

For God, who commanded the light to shine out of darkness, hath shined in our hearts, to [give] the light of the knowledge of the glory of God in the face of Jesus Christ. —II Cor. 4:6

As a believer, God's Word is engrafted in me. I will, by His Word, celebrate His Life working in me. I will continue in His Word, being a doer of the Word and not a hearer only. The Holy Spirit will grow the *law of liberty* in me from *glory to glory* (level to level) as I increasingly reflect the face of God. Just as Jesus was a reflection of God's face (His glory, His character), so will I become that reflection as I mature in Him. I will know grace and peace magnified in my life, becoming all that God intends me to be.

Confession – Day Twenty-Eight

And I say also unto thee, That thou art Peter, and upon this rock I will build my church; and the gates of hell shall not prevail against it. Again I say unto you, That if two of you shall agree on earth as touching any thing that they shall ask, it shall be done for them of my Father which is in heaven. —Mat 16:18-19

No weapon that is formed against thee shall prosper; and every tongue [that] shall rise against thee in judgment thou shalt condemn. This [is] the heritage of the servants of the LORD, and their righteousness [is] of me, saith the LORD. —Isaiah 54:17

Finally, my brethren, be strong in the Lord, and in the power of his might. Put on the whole armor of God, that ye may be able to stand against the wiles of the devil. For we wrestle not against flesh and blood, but against principalities, against powers, against the rulers of the darkness of this world, against spiritual wickedness in high [places]. Wherefore take unto you the whole armor of God, that ye may be able to withstand in the evil day, and having done all, to stand. Stand therefore, having your loins girt about with truth, and having on the breastplate of righteousness; And your feet shod with the preparation of the gospel of peace; Above all, taking the shield of faith, wherewith ye shall be able to quench all the fiery darts of the wicked. And take the helmet of salvation, and the sword of the Spirit, which is the word of God: Praying always with all prayer and supplication in the Spirit, and watching thereunto with all perseverance and supplication for all saints; -Eph. 6:10-18

I can do all things through Christ which strengtheneth me. –Phil.4:13

I will put on and wear the full armor of God, refusing to make myself vulnerable to the fiery darts of the wicked one, Satan. My battle is not with flesh and blood. My enemy is Satan and no weapon he forms against me will prosper when I am wearing the full armor of God. Not even the gates of hell can defeat me as I walk in the Spirit of God. I am more than a conqueror in Christ and will remain in Him where I can accomplish anything to His glory!

Confession – Day Twenty-Nine

My brethren, count it all joy when ye fall into divers temptations; Knowing [this], that the trying of your faith worketh patience. But let patience have [her] perfect work, that ye may be perfect and entire, wanting nothing. –James 1: 2-4

Not that I speak in respect of want: for I have learned, in whatsoever state I am, [therewith] to be content. –Phil. 4:11

But they that wait upon the LORD shall renew [their] strength; they shall mount up with wings as eagles; they shall run, and not be weary; [and] they shall walk, and not faint. —Is. 40:31

I refuse to walk in restlessness or discontent. Regardless of the circumstances of my life, I will joy in the Lord. His joy is my strength. When struggles come, I will rejoice and wait upon the Lord, knowing that the working of my patience brings completion or fullness to my Christian life. When tests or trials come, I am confident God will use them to stretch me, to increase my capacities, to grow me in trusting Him. I will know God's purpose, His power, His pleasure and His peace. I am not content to remain a baby in Christ but will, by His Spirit, grow into the maturity of His calling in my life.

Confession – Day Thirty

And if one prevail against him, two shall withstand him; and a threefold cord is not quickly broken. —Ecc. 4:12

For where two or three are gathered together in my name, there am I in the midst of them. —Matthew 18:20

Behold, how good and how pleasant [it is] for brethren to dwell together in unity! [It is] like the precious ointment upon the head, that ran down upon the beard, [even] Aaron's beard: that went down to the skirts of his garments; As the dew of Hermon, [and as the dew] that descended upon the mountains of Zion: for there the LORD commanded the blessing, [even] life for evermore. —Psalm 133:1-3

I can do all things through Christ which strengtheneth me. —Phil. 4:13

And he said unto me, My grace is sufficient for thee: for my strength is made perfect in weakness. Most gladly therefore will I rather glory in my infirmities, that the power of Christ may rest upon me. —II Cor. 12:9

My role model for unity is the Trinity. God the Father, Jesus the Son, and Holy Spirit work in perfect harmony. Out of the harmony came all of creation and in that harmony, all creation is held together. I will walk in unity with God (His Word) and with my fellow believers. As the mind of Christ is perfected in me and the love of God grows more perfect in me, I will find the unity of God's unlimited power. I will walk in the commanded blessing of God. With God, nothing is impossible. If God be for me, who can be against me! I am limited only as I limit my agreement with God. I choose to believe His Word completely, finding purpose, power and peace in the Kingdom. In myself, I am weak. As I humble myself in unity with God, I am strong in His strength. His grace is sufficient for me in every situation of life. I am indeed more than a conqueror in Christ.

Confession – Day Thirty-One

It is written: "I believed; therefore I have spoken."With that same spirit of faith we also believe and therefore speak, because we know that the one who raised the Lord Jesus from the dead will also raise us with Jesus and present us with you in his presence. All this is for your benefit, so that the grace that is reaching more and more people may cause thanksgiving to overflow to the glory of God. -II Cor. 4:13-15

Wherefore thou art no more a servant, but a son; and if a son, then an heir of God through Christ.   - Gal. 4:7

The Spirit of the Lord [is] upon me, because he hath anointed me to preach the gospel to the poor; he hath sent me to heal the brokenhearted, to preach deliverance to the captives, and recovering of sight to the blind, to set at liberty them that are bruised, To preach the acceptable year of the Lord. –Luke 4:18-19

Verily, verily, I say unto you, He that believeth on me, the works that I do shall he do also; and greater [works] than these shall he do; because I go unto my Father. –John 14:12

And he ordained twelve, that they should be with him, and that he might send them forth to preach, And to have power to heal sicknesses, and to cast out devils: -Mark 3:14-15

The Spirit of the Lord is upon me. I am a joint heir with Jesus and have the same Father. I have been given the keys to the Kingdom! All the resources of the Father's "house" are available to me. I am a disciple of the living Lord Jesus and am commissioned to preach the gospel, to heal the sick, to set the captives free. As I grow in God's love, He can trust me with authority to do great things in His name, to His glory. I live not for self but for the glory of God. My life is hidden in Him.

Confession – Write Your Own

Now that you have completed thirty-one confessions, write your own. Purchase a spiral notebook and write one of your struggles or goals at the top of the page. Next, find and list appropriate scriptures-Kingdom Truths-which apply to your need. Finally, write your faith confession. Do this routinely and see your spirit soar!

We will be glad to pray for you. Simply access spiritlifejourney.com on the internet, and click on the PRAYER NEEDS icon.

Perhaps you will be led of the Spirit to form a Spirit-Life study group. For more information, access spiritlifejourney.com and click on the STUDY GROUP icon.